Themes From A to Z

26 Cross-Curricular Theme Units

Preschool–Kindergarten

D1621815

Editors:
Cindy K. Daoust
Ada Goren
Sherri Lynn Kuntz
Mackie Rhodes
Jan Trautman
Susan Walker

Artists:
Pam Crane
Teresa R. Davidson
Theresa Lewis Goode
Nick Greenwood
Sheila Krill
Mary Lester
Kimberly Richard
Greg D. Rieves
Rebecca Saunders
Barry Slate
Donna K. Teal

Cover Artists:
Nick Greenwood
Kimberly Richard

www.themailbox.com

©2000 by THE EDUCATION CENTER, INC.
All rights reserved.
ISBN #1-56234-416-1

Manufactured in the United States

10 9 8 7 6 5 4

Table of Contents

Alligators All Around

Your students will get giddy over gators—and learn a whole lot—with the activities in this cross-curricular unit. So slide right in—it's time for alligators!

ideas by Suzanne Moore

What We Know
- I know that alligators can swim. Sherri
- They ha... Ricky
- They lo... me. Shawn
- Alligators... saw that
- Th...

What We Want to Know
- Why do they live in swamps? Nicholas
- Why do they float in the water? Trevor
- How much do th... ?
- Do they com...t? Yianni
- How bi...
- w... gs? Keesha
- ...they Dakot...

What We Learned
- Alligators swim and float. Aaron
- They have scales all over their bodies! Kevi...
- They roar sometimes a... e... hiss. Yianni
- ...ies h... fi...

Getting Acquainted

Lure your little ones into alligator territory with this activity. In advance, create three poster board swamp scenes as shown. Glue a copy of the alligator pattern on page 7 to each of the swamp posters. Program the posters as indicated and then hang them on a bulletin board at students' eye level. Begin a class discussion about alligators and have each child tell what he already knows about alligators and what he wants to learn about them. Record responses on the appropriate posters. Then read *Waiting Alligators* by William Muñoz (Lerner Publications Company). Encourage students to signal (by snapping, touching shoulders, raising hands, etc.) when they hear a new fact in the story. Print student responses on the third swamp poster. Encourage students to add new discoveries and questions to the posters throughout the unit. Gosh, gators are interesting!

Ode to Alligators

Science, language skills, and humor combine to create a gator-sized learning opportunity in this poem. In advance, copy the poem (right) on chart paper. Practice reading it together, encouraging children to make up appropriate actions. Then have students interact with the print as they are able. For example, have children take turns underlining the word *alligator* with a green marker. Or invite different students to circle the rhyming word pairs in each stanza. Afterward, display the poem at child height, encouraging children to include it in their read-the-room routines. Go, gators!

Ode to Alligators

Alligators swim
And alligators slide.
Alligators open their jaws very wide!

Alligators hunt
And alligators eat.
Alligators think big birds are a treat!

Alligators grumble
And alligators roar.
I wonder if an alligator's throat gets sore!

Alligators snap
And an alligator nips.
I'll *never* kiss an alligator on the lips!

—*adapted from a poem by Suzanne Moore*

? Did You Know?
An alligator's ears are hidden inside flaps of skin behind its eyes.

That's About the Size of 'em

Exactly how big *are* alligators? Amaze your youngsters with life-size alligator cutouts to explore! Duplicate the alligator pattern on page 7 and then use an overhead projector to enlarge the pattern to match the sizes listed. Use a permanent marker to trace each enlarged projection onto a piece of white poster board (tape several pieces together if necessary). Have students sponge-paint the gators green, blue-gray, or black. Cut the alligators out and display them on a wall close to the floor (a hallway wall works well). Facilitate a discussion about how alligators continue to grow their entire lives while humans stop growing when they reach adulthood. Then ask each child to compare the size of each alligator to her own size. Have each child use classroom items—such as paper clips, toy cars, and markers—to measure the length of the alligators.

Approximate alligator sizes:
newly hatched = 9 inches long
1 year old = 2 feet long
3 years old = 4 feet long
5 years old = 6 feet long
adult female = 9 feet long
adult male = 13 feet long

? Did You Know?
Alligators can grow up to 20 feet in length!

Step 1: Draw an oval. This is the alligator's body.

Step 2: Draw a long triangle tail touching the body.

Step 3: Draw a triangle to resemble the alligator's head. Add details, such as an eye, a nostril, a mouth, and teeth.

Step 4: Draw four square legs. Add claws.

Alligator Art

Submerge your young artists in a pool of learning with this shape art project! Use the steps shown to guide each student in drawing and coloring an alligator on a sheet of white construction paper. Then have students draw pools of water around their alligators, making sure their nostrils and eyes are peeking out. Also invite students to draw other animals and details, such as turtles, fish, birds, the sun, and plants. Print the word *alligator* on the board and encourage students to write it on their drawings. As an extension activity, have each student cut out paper shapes to glue together to resemble an alligator. Hang the gators on a bulletin board for a wild wetland display!

Five Baby Alligators

Crack! Five cute gators emerge from their eggs to help your little ones reinforce beginning math skills! Beforehand, make five poster board copies of the baby alligator puppet pattern on page 7. Color and then cut out the gators. Cut out the eyeholes where indicated. Use a glue stick to attach a black hole-punch eye on each of two fingers of five student volunteers. Then have the volunteers slip their dotted fingers through the eyeholes in the alligators. As the class chants the poem, have students use the puppets to act it out. Repeat until every child has had a turn to use a puppet. Place the gator puppets at a center for more dramatic play. Aren't these gators great?

Five Baby Alligators

Five baby alligators hiss, bellow, and roar.
One swam away and then there were four.

Four baby alligators happy as can be.
One swam away and then there were three.

Three baby alligators grew and grew and grew.
One swam away and then there were two.

Two baby alligators basking in the sun.
One swam away and then there was one.

One baby alligator didn't want to stay.
Snap went his mouth and he swam away.

Alligator Authors

Good golly, a gator book! Your group will be grinning from ear to ear as students work cooperatively to make this class book. To prepare, enlarge the alligator pattern on page 7 and copy it onto green construction paper for a book cover. After cutting the cover out, use it as a template to make a class supply of construction paper pages. Instruct each student to draw an alligator and its habitat on his page. Then ask a child what he would do if he were an alligator. Write his response on his page. When the pages are complete, stack them behind the cover and bind the book together. If desired, add a wiggle eye to the book cover. After reading the book together, put it in your reading area. Your youngsters will hunt for it again and again!

Green Gator Gulp

Gabbing about gators can make your group thirsty! This green gator drink is sure to refresh your little ones, especially when they help you create it. To make 16 to 20 servings, combine one large can of pineapple juice and one liter of 7-Up® or Sprite® in a punch bowl. Add a half gallon of lime sherbet and allow it to melt for a few minutes. Grab a gator book from the list below and read aloud while your youngsters enjoy their gator drink. Gulp, gulp, gone!

Grab a Gator Book!

Nonfiction

The Alligator
By Sabrina Crewe
Illustrated by Jim Chanell
Published by Raintree Steck-Vaughn Publishers

Alligators
By Frank Staub
Published by Lerner Publications Company

Never Kiss an Alligator
By Colleen Stanley Bare
Published by Cobblehill Books

Fiction

An Extraordinary Egg
By Leo Lionni
Published by Dragonfly Books

Feliciana Feydra Le Roux: A Cajun Tall Tale
By Tynia Thomassie
Illustrated by Cat Bowman Smith
Published by Little, Brown and Company

For Pete's Sake
By Ellen Stoll Walsh
Published by Harcourt Brace & Company

Gertie and Gumbo
By Matt Novak
Published by Orchard Books

There's an Alligator Under My Bed
By Mercer Mayer
Published by Dial Books for Young Readers

Did You Know?
Alligators have a third eyelid that is see-through. They shut only this third eyelid when they're underwater so they can see!

Alligator Pattern
Use with the alligator activities on pages 4–6.

Alligator Puppet Pattern
Use with "Five Baby Alligators" on page 5.

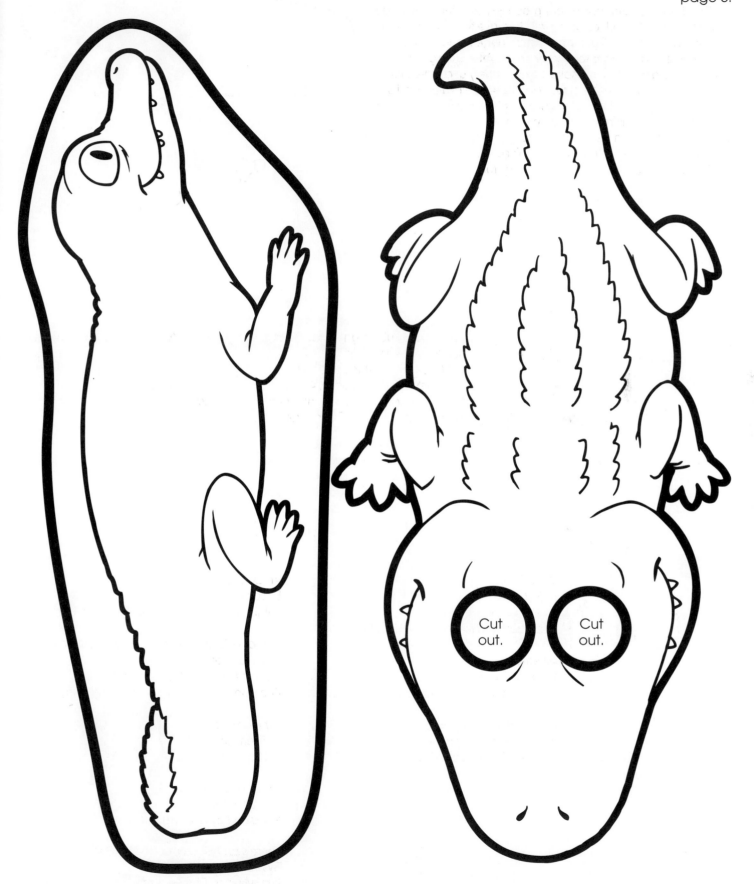

Cut out.   Cut out.

A Bounty of Berries

Berries are beautiful and berries taste fine.
Pick 'em from the store, the fridge, or the vine!

Explore the wonders of berries with these activities picked especially for you.

ideas by Bambina L. Merriman

A Taste Test

Introduce youngsters to a variety of berries with this yummy math activity. In advance, ask several parents to each donate a basket of strawberries, blueberries, blackberries, or raspberries. (If fresh berries are not in season, request frozen ones.) Then prepare a chart similar to the one shown. To begin, give each student the same type of berry. Encourage him to examine the berry and to share his observations about its appearance, texture, and smell. Then invite each child to taste his berry. Repeat the activity for each berry type. Then have each child put a sticky dot on the graph to indicate which berry he likes best. Which berry is the class favorite? Second favorite? Third favorite? Least favorite?

Juicy, Juicy!

Use this irresistible hands-on idea to squeeze a little science into your berry explorations. For every four students, ask a different parent to send in a pint of raspberries (or a bag of frozen ones). Then ask several other parents to each send in a jar of cranberry juice. On the appointed day, gather a class supply of plastic bowls, spoons, and paper cups, as well as a few plastic potato mashers, $1/2$-cup measuring cups, and some strainers. Ask youngsters to predict what will happen to a raspberry if it is mashed. After sharing their responses, have each child measure $1/2$ cup of raspberries into a bowl. Have her mash her berries with a potato masher. What happens? Then help her strain the liquid into a cup. Next, invite her to stir in $1/2$ cup of cranberry juice to create a juicy-juicy drink. Mmmm! Lip-smacking good!

Pick a Pail of Berries

Imaginations and movement blend perfectly to pack a bale of fun into this activity.

Pick a Pail of Berries
(sung to the tune of "Pick a Bale of Cotton")

Jump down, turn around,
Pick a bunch of [strawberries].
Jump down, turn around,
Put 'em in the pail.
(Repeat verse.)

Chorus:
Oh, [stretch]!
Pick a bunch of [strawberries].
Oh, [stretch]!
Put 'em in the pail.

Each time you repeat the song, replace *strawberries* with a different berry name and *stretch* with a different action word, such as *bend, kneel,* or *skip.*

Bushels of Berries

Invite youngsters to make lots and lots of manipulative berries to stock your math and dramatic-play centers. (For center activities, see "Berry Count" on this page and "Berry Buys" on page 10.) For each different berry type, use the recipe below to make a batch of dough in the appropriate color. Then divide your class into groups equal to the number of batches of dough. Have each group make berries out of its assigned dough. As students shape blueberries, blackberries, raspberries, and strawberries, have them texture their berries by gently poking them with plastic forks or pencils. After the berries air-dry (several days), have youngsters dot seeds onto the strawberries with black fine-tipped permanent markers.

Berry Count

Count on this activity to reinforce a bushel of math skills and fine-motor practice. To begin, cut the lid off an egg carton. Use a permanent marker to label each egg cup with a numeral from 1 to 12. Store a supply of blueberries (made in "Bushels of Berries") in a basket. Place the basket of blueberries, a pair of plastic tweezers, and the counting tray in your math center. To do this activity, each child uses the tweezers to transfer the appropriate number of berries into each cup. If desired, try this activity with real blueberries. Ready, set, count!

Berry Dough
(Makes about 30 actual-size berries.)

2 c. flour
$3/4$ c. salt
$1/2$ tsp. alum
$1/3$ c. of black, blue, red, or pink tempera paint
water

Combine the dry ingredients. Mix water with the paint color of your choice to make $3/4$ cup liquid. Slowly add the liquid to the dry ingredients, mixing until a dough forms. Add more water or flour as needed until you have the desired consistency. Knead the dough well.

Berry Buys

Promote your youngsters' purchasing savvy with this produce stand that is stocked with berries, berries, and more berries. To prepare, copy and cut out a supply of green construction paper berry bucks (page 11). Then set up your dramatic-play center to resemble a berry stand. Put the dough berries (from "Bushels of Berries" on page 9) into assorted containers; then label each container with a dollar amount. Display the containers on the stand along with a toy cash register. Then add berry baskets, paper bags, wallets (envelopes), and the berry bucks to the center. Invite small groups of students to role-play buyers and attendants at the stand. Encourage youngsters to rotate roles so that each child plays each part. Before leaving the center, have students sort and return all the items to the stand for the next group.

blueberries

strawberries

raspberries

$2.00

$3.00

$1.00

A Bevy of Berries

Fill a sensory tub with mounds of cereal berries to provide youngsters with some sensory sensations. In advance, ask parents to donate boxes of berry-flavored cereal, such as Cap'n Crunch's® Oops! All Berries™ cereal. Pour the cereal into the sensory tub. (If desired, save some cereal for snacktime!) Then add scoops, ladles, measuring cups, and small bowls. Invite youngsters to use the supplies to explore measurement and counting skills. Dig in!

"Berry" Good Reading

Blueberries for Sal
By Robert McCloskey
Published by Viking

The Grey Lady and the Strawberry Snatcher
By Molly Bang
Published by Aladdin Paperbacks

Jamberry
By Bruce Degen
Published by HarperTrophy

The Little Mouse, the Red Ripe Strawberry, and the Big Hungry Bear
By Don and Audrey Wood
Illustrated by Don Wood
Published by Child's Play (International) Ltd

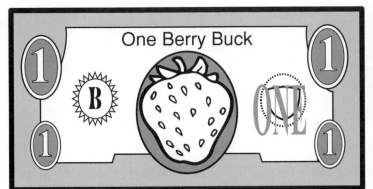

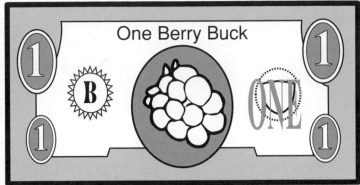

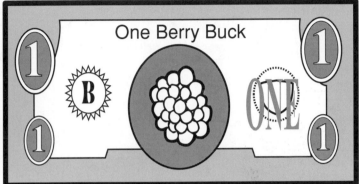

©2000 The Education Center, Inc. • *Themes From A to Z* • TEC373

Dear Parent,

Our class has had a great time learning with berries! And you can continue the fun at home! Use berries for counting and sorting activities with your child. Or join your child in large-muscle movements (exercise!) as you pick imaginary berries. Here's a simple rhyme to say with your child. Have fun!

B is for berries—
Black and blue.
Raspberries, strawberries,
Cranberries, too.

B is for berries—
For me and you.
Pick berries, count berries,
Eat berries, too!

©2000 The Education Center, Inc. • *Themes From A to Z* • TEC373

Note to the teacher: At the end of your berry studies, send a copy of this parent letter home with each child.

Bb 11

Castles, Castles Everywhere

Hear ye! Hear ye! Let it be known to all that these colossal castle activities provide royal learning opportunities for the little lords and ladies of your classroom kingdom!

ideas by Vicki Dabrowka

Castle Vocabulary

- A water-filled ditch around a castle is called a *moat*.
- A *drawbridge* is a bridge that can be raised or lowered over the moat.
- The *gatehouse* includes the towers and gates at the entrance of the castle.
- A *portcullis* is a heavy sliding gate.
- The *great hall* is a large room used for business and banquets.
- *Loopholes* are small openings in the castle walls through which weapons were fired.
- The *keep* is a stone tower in the middle of the castle.

The Royal Residence

Build your students' castle knowledge and vocabulary with a close-up view of these magnificent structures. To begin, share some realistic castle illustrations from books such as *Castles* by Philip Steele (Kingfisher) or *A Medieval Castle* by Fiona Macdonald and illustrated by Mark Bergin (Peter Bedrick Books). As you explore the pictures together, use the vocabulary guide below to point out the different parts and functions of a castle. Then invite youngsters to share their thoughts and ideas about castles and castle life.

Classroom Castle

After your students have been introduced to castle architecture, invite them to create their own classroom castle! To prepare, collect a large appliance box and an assortment of other boxes. Cut the appliance box to resemble the castle *keep*. Put the keep in a center area along with your box collection, masking tape, paint, and markers. Then invite small groups to build and decorate additions to the castle. When the castle is complete, add dress-up clothes and props to the center. Then let the royal role-playing begin!

Royal Subjects

Familiarize your students with some of the people from the days of castles. To prepare, color and cut out two copies of the castle character cards on page 15; then back them with tagboard. Next, tell students that the inhabitants and visitors of a castle included many different people. Show them a card for each castle character, using the list at right for reference. Afterward, keep the cards in a learning center and invite small groups to use them to play a memory game.

- A *lord* was the castle owner.
- A *lady* was the wife of the lord.
- A *knight* fought on horseback.
- A *page* was a young boy training to become a knight.
- A *falconer* trained eagles, falcons, and hawks to hunt food.
- A *jester's* job was to make people laugh, *jugglers* entertained the household, and *minstrels* sung and played music for dancing.

Castle Characters Graph

Who would *you* like to be if you lived during castle times? To prepare for this activity, copy and cut apart the castle character cards on page 15. Also reduce the castle pattern on page 15 and make a class supply. Then label a graph with each card as shown. Ask each child to cut out her castle pattern and label it with her name. During a group time, pose the above question; then invite each child to tape her castle onto the graph to indicate her choice. What does the graph reveal about your classroom castle characters?

Character Creations

Promote creative expression when you invite each child to make a character corresponding to his choice in "Castle Characters Graph." To make the body, have each child fold a sheet of construction paper in half lengthwise. Then have him fold it in thirds as shown. Next, instruct him to unfold his paper and cut off the bottom corner sections to create a T shape. Then have the child glue a construction paper head, hands, and feet onto the body. Invite him to use a variety of craft items to decorate the clothing and add accessories to his character. Display all of the creations with the title "Our Castle Characters."

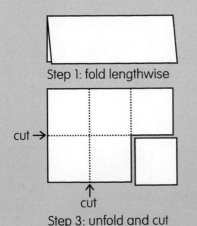

Step 1: fold lengthwise

Step 2: fold in thirds

cut →

↑ cut

Step 3: unfold and cut corner sections

Step 3: after cutting a T shape.

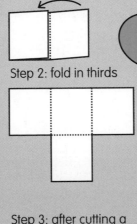

Middle Ages Melody

Teach youngsters this song to reinforce the castle character names learned in "Royal Subjects" (page 13). Have children join hands in a standing circle. Then appoint a child to be the castle lord and stand in the middle of the circle. Sing the song at right in the same way you'd sing (and act out) "The Farmer in the Dell." Continue in this manner, naming different characters each time you sing the second verse. To conclude the game, insert *wizard* for the last underlined word in each line. At this time, the wizard taps each character in the circle to make him "disappear" from the castle! Play several rounds to give every child a turn to play a role.

(sung to the tune of "The Farmer in the Dell")

The lord is in the castle.　　The [lord] takes a [lady].
The lord is in the castle.　　The [lord] takes a [lady].
Heigh-ho, the derry-oh,　　Heigh-ho, the derry-oh,
The lord is in the castle.　　The [lord] takes a [lady].

Each time you repeat the second verse, replace the second underlined word in each line with *knight, page, falconer, jester, juggler,* or *minstrel.*

Sand Castles

Invite each of your royal subjects to create her own castle—with sand! To prepare, enlarge the castle pattern on page 15; then make one tagboard copy for each child. Put the patterns in your art center along with shakers of sand. Have each child color her castle. Then instruct her to trace some of the castle lines with glue or to draw on her own glue details and designs on the castle. Then have the child sprinkle sand onto the glue and shake off the excess sand. After the sand castles dry, display them with the projects made in "Character Creations" (page 13).

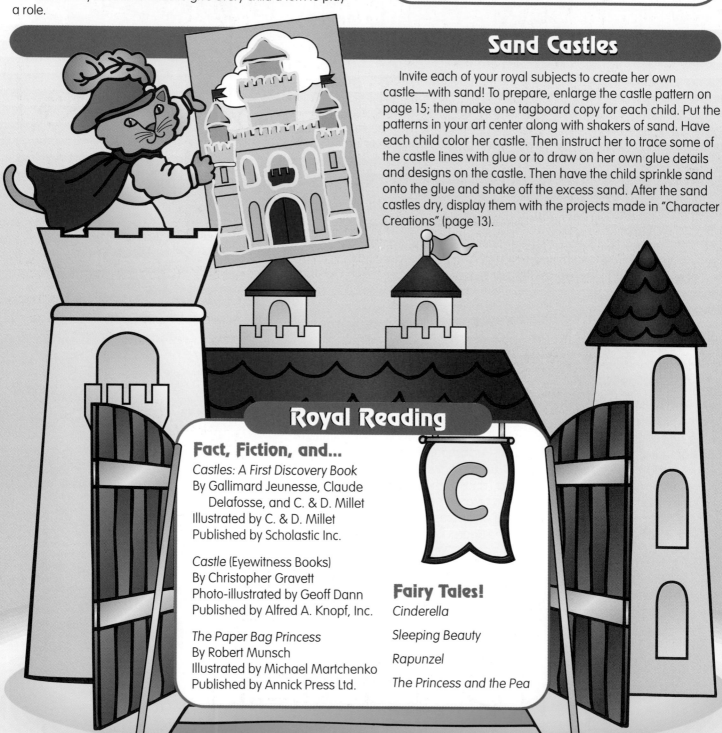

Royal Reading

Fact, Fiction, and...

Castles: A First Discovery Book
By Gallimard Jeunesse, Claude
　　Delafosse, and C. & D. Millet
Illustrated by C. & D. Millet
Published by Scholastic Inc.

Castle (Eyewitness Books)
By Christopher Gravett
Photo-illustrated by Geoff Dann
Published by Alfred A. Knopf, Inc.

The Paper Bag Princess
By Robert Munsch
Illustrated by Michael Martchenko
Published by Annick Press Ltd.

Fairy Tales!

Cinderella

Sleeping Beauty

Rapunzel

The Princess and the Pea

lord

lady

knight

page

falconer

jester

juggler

minstrel

Castle Pattern
Use with "Castle Characters Graph" on page 13 and "Sand Castles" on page 14.

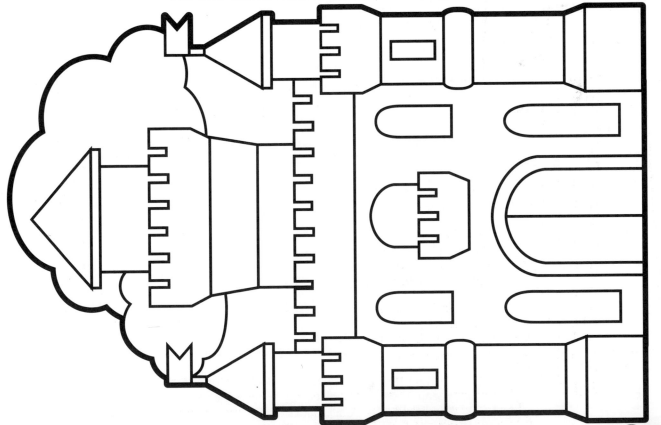

Make Way for Ducks!

Use these dandy duck ideas to introduce your youngsters to the delightful world of ducks.

ideas by Diane Gilliam

Duck Details

Introduce your study of these fine-feathered friends with this ducky display. Cut out three large bulletin board paper ducks. Title one duck "What We Know About Ducks," the second "What We Want to Know About Ducks," and the third "What We Learned About Ducks." Display the ducks on a wall. Then encourage youngsters to share facts that they already know about ducks. Write their responses on the first duck. Next, ask students what they would *like* to know about ducks and record those comments on the second duck. Then share *Ducks Don't Get Wet* by Augusta Goldin (HarperCollins Publishers). After discussing the book, ask students to recall the duck facts they learned from the book. Write their responses on the third duck. Then, as you continue your study of ducks, add new facts and discoveries as they occur.

What We Know About Ducks
- Ducks have feathers.
- Ducks can swim.
- Ducks can fly.

What We Want to Know About Ducks
- How do ducks stay dry?
- What do ducks eat?
- Why do ducks fly away when it's cold?

What We Learned About Ducks
- Ducks keep their feathers waterproof by preening.
- Ducks migrate to warm places to find food.
- A baby duck is a duckling.

When I preen, I spread a special oil all over my feathers to keep them waterproof.

In the winter, I migrate to warm climates so I can find food.

I use my webbed feet to paddle around the water while I look for food.

A Little Duck Ditty

Reinforce rhyme and vocabulary with this duck-related action poem.

The daddy **drake,** mama **duck,**	Spread arms; then bring them closer together.
And baby **duckling** new	Cup hands.
Have two webbed feet	Hold up two fingers.
And oily feathers, too.	Slide palm down chest.
Ducks **waddle** on the land.	Waddle and flap "wings."
They **waddle** to and fro.	
And when they're in the water	Step forward.
They paddle as they go!	Paddle hands in front of body.
But when the winter comes,	Shiver.
Away the ducks will fly.	Flap "wings."
They **migrate** to warm places	
While winter passes by.	Move arms over head from one side to other.
But they'll be back in springtime,	Arc arms to make a sun.
Preening every little feather.	Pretend to preen.
Waddle, waddle. Quack, quack.	Imitate a duck.
How ducks do love warm weather!	

Migration Stations

Youngsters will eagerly flock to this tasty migration activity. In advance, gather five or six different kinds of dry snack foods, such as popcorn, cereal, and crackers. Put each one in a separate bowl with a scoop. Just before a group time, set up migration stations by placing the bowls in one general area of your room. (It would be great if it's convenient to put the snack bowls in a *southern* section of your room!) Also, post a large construction paper sun in that area. During group time, explain that when winter weather arrives, ducks *migrate* to warmer regions. Ask children to share why they think this happens. Lead them to conclude that cold temperatures freeze the water, making it difficult for ducks to find food. To reinforce the concept of migration, invite children to pretend to be ducks in the following activity.

To begin, divide your class of ducks into thirds. Give each duck a plastic bag. Explain that most of your classroom is experiencing a very cold pretend winter at the moment. Then invite each group of ducks, in turn, to migrate to warmer weather where the food is abundant. Invite each duck to collect a little food from each bowl. After a short time, signal that flock of ducks to quietly fly to tables for a snack!

Ducks on Display

For each child you will need:
12" white circle
tracers for the duck head and
    feet (see note)
craft feathers
newspaper strips
white and orange construction
    paper
assorted paint colors
scissors
glue
marker

Your students will quack at the chance to decorate your classroom with these designer ducks! To make a duck, trace the duck head on white paper and the duck foot twice on orange paper. Cut out the shapes. Next, use a feather to paint both sides of the circle and both sides of the duck head. When the paint is dry, fold the circle in half with the unpainted sides together and then cut a 2¼-inch slit along the fold. Then insert and glue the head between the slit. Leaving an opening at one end, glue the edges of the body together and insert the feet between them. Finally, stuff the duck with newspaper strips, glue the opening closed, and draw an eye on each side of the duck. Mount all the ducks on a board and encourage children to use art supplies to create a habitat to surround their ducks on display.

Note: To make tracers for the duck head and feet, make tagboard copies of the corresponding patterns on page 19.

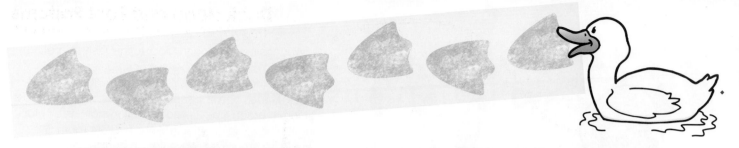

Duck Tracks

These webbed footprint designs can be used as headbands, nameplates for your youngsters' masterpieces, or as a display border. To make a sponge printer, trace the duck footprint pattern (page 19) onto a craft sponge. Cut out the shape; then hot-glue a soda bottle lid to it to use as a handle. Expand the sponge with water and set it aside to dry. Then invite each child to sponge-print duck footprints across a strip of construction paper. To use the work as a nameplate, have each child label a small strip of paper with her name and then glue it on the printed strip. Display each child's nameplate with her duck from "Ducks on Display." Or, if desired, encourage each child to make several duck-print strips; then use them to border your duck-related displays.

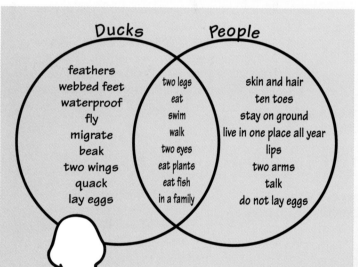

Ducks | People

feathers
webbed feet
waterproof
fly
migrate
beak
two wings
quack
lay eggs

two legs
eat
swim
walk
two eyes
eat plants
eat fish
in a family

skin and hair
ten toes
stay on ground
live in one place all year
lips
two arms
talk
do not lay eggs

We Are Alike, We Are Different

How are ducks and people alike and different? Well, let's see! To begin, draw two large overlapping circles on a sheet of bulletin board paper. Write "Ducks" above one circle and "People" above the other. Then ask youngsters to compare ducks and people. Write the responses that apply only to ducks or only to people in the corresponding circles. List the attributes that are shared by both groups in the middle. Afterward—just for fun—ask each child to draw a duck-person by combining several characteristics from each group. Then invite him to share his creative picture with the class.

Duck Tales

Come Along, Daisy!
By Jane Simmons
Published by Little, Brown and Company

Farmer Duck
By Martin Waddell
Illustrated by Helen Oxenbury
Published by Candlewick Press

Five Little Ducks
By Raffi
Illustrated by Jose Aruego and Ariane Dewey
Published by Crown Publishers, Inc.

Happy Birthday, Dear Duck
By Eve Bunting
Illustrated by Jan Brett
Published by Clarion Books

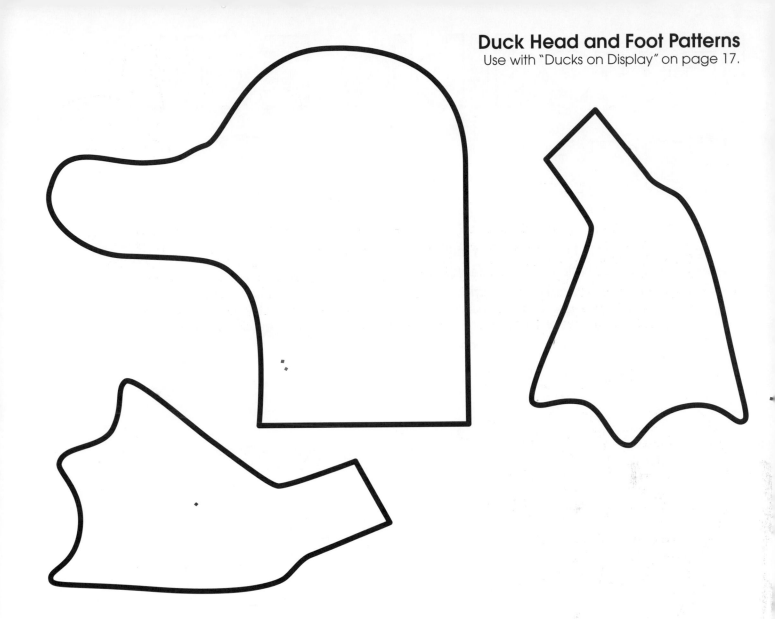

Duck Head and Foot Patterns
Use with "Ducks on Display" on page 17.

Duck Footprint Patterns
Use with "Duck Tracks" on page 18.

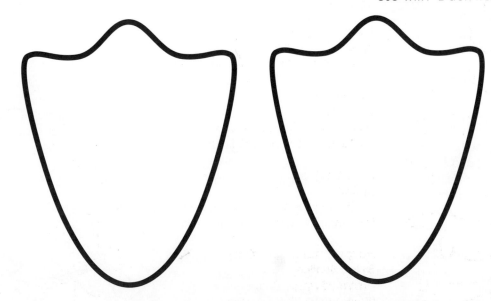

Incredible Edible Eggs

"Eggs-tra! Eggs-tra!" Learn all about 'em!
These egg-related activities will provide youngsters with some extraordinary information about
these oval-shaped wonders.

ideas contributed by Linda Gordetsky

Green Eggs Here, Green Eggs There

Many of your students will easily identify with the character in *Green Eggs and Ham* by Dr. Seuss (Random House, Inc.). Read this rhyming classic to youngsters; then ask them why the character might have been reluctant to taste green eggs and ham. Discuss what happened when the character finally tried the green foods. Afterward, ask each child to draw a picture of two situations in which he *might* eat green eggs and ham—all rhyming is welcome! Then label each picture with the child's dictation. To make a class book, staple the pages between two construction paper covers. Title the book "We Do So Like Them!" Then invite each child to read his page to the class. Later, put the book in your reading center for a free-time reading option.

Eggs and the Fixin's

Introduce youngsters to some different styles of cooked eggs; then invite them to create egg platters with their favorite fixin's. In advance, prepare one egg in each of these cooking methods: scrambled, hard-boiled, sunny-side up, and over easy. Show your class the eggs. Ask students if they know the different name for how each egg is prepared. After establishing the egg names, invite youngsters to tell about their favorite egg styles and side fixin's. Then give each child a paper plate. Ask her to use craft supplies to illustrate her plate with her preferred egg style. Then have her glue magazine and ad cutouts to her plate to show some of her favorite egg fixin's. (Or have her draw her own pictures.) During group time, invite each child to share her egg platter with the class.

Chef Says...

Your youngsters will scramble to play this adapted version of Simon Says. First, tell them that whether an egg is scrambled, hard-boiled, sunny-side up, or over easy, it has its own characteristics. Then discuss the different looks of each egg style from "Eggs and the Fixin's" (page 20). Afterward, invite students to play the game. To begin, practice the position (described below) for each egg style. Appoint one child to be the chef and the others to be eggs. To play, the eggs sit on the platter (a large open area). Then the chef names one of the four egg styles. If he says "Chef says" first, each egg will position himself accordingly. If the chef does not say "Chef says," the eggs do not move. If an egg does move, he sits out for one round of play. Periodically, appoint a different child to be the chef. Continue play as long as student interest dictates.

- Scrambled: Crouch down to form a mound with your body.
- Hard-boiled: Sit and wrap your arms tightly around your knees.
- Sunny-side up: Lie flat on your back.
- Over easy: Lie flat on your stomach.

Eggs Everywhere

Where do eggs come from? Invite your students to share their answers to this question. Then tell them that the eggs we are most familiar with come from chickens. But chickens are not the only animals that lay eggs. To illustrate this, read aloud *Chickens Aren't the Only Ones* by Ruth Heller (Grosset & Dunlap, Inc.). After discussing the different egg-laying animals in the book, teach youngsters the song below. Each time you repeat the song, replace the underlined word with a different egg-laying animal, using the book as a reference.

Egg Song

(sung to the tune of "Old McDonald")

[Chickens] lay eggs,
This we know.
E-I-E-I-O.
And from those eggs
[Chickens] grow.
E-I-E-I-O.

There's a [chicken] egg here
And a [chicken] egg there.
Here an egg, there an egg,
Everywhere a [chicken] egg.

[Chickens] lay eggs,
This we know.
E-I-E-I-O.

Egg Race

Play this simple board game with your youngsters to reinforce some of the different egg-laying animals. To prepare, make a gameboard similar to the one shown and provide several game markers (such as cubes or dried beans). Then color and cut out two tagboard copies of the animal cards on page 23. Shuffle the cards and stack them on the gameboard. For rewards, put treat-filled plastic eggs in a basket near the gameboard.

To play the game, each child, in turn, draws a card from the deck. If the card shows an egg-laying animal, the player advances her game marker to the next egg space. Then she flips a penny to determine how many more spaces to move—one space for heads and two for tails. If the card does not show an egg-laying animal, the child doesn't move to the next egg space, but flips the penny and moves the corresponding number of spaces. When a player reaches "Finish," she picks an egg from the basket and "cracks" it open to discover the surprise inside.

"Egg-ceptional" Centers

Help students practice a variety of basic concepts with these center activities. To begin, collect a supply of plastic eggs and egg cartons; then prepare them for each activity as described.

- Label each of 26 eggs with a different letter. Have students sequence sets of 12 eggs in an egg carton. Or tape egg-cup strips together to create a 26-cup strip; then have students sequence the eggs in the long strip.

- Label each of 12 eggs with a numeral from 1 to 12. Instruct each child to sequence the eggs in an egg carton.

- Put an assortment of egg sizes in a basket; then label a different egg carton for each size represented (such as "small," "medium," and "large"). Have each child sort the eggs into the appropriate cartons.

- Place a basket of colorful eggs in a center along with an egg carton labeled for each color. Invite each child to sort the eggs by color. Increase the fine-motor fun by asking children to use a spoon to transfer each egg from the basket to the carton.

Read All About Eggs

Daisy and the Egg
by Jane Simmons
Published by Little, Brown and Company

Egg: A Photographic Story of Hatching
By Robert Burton
Photographed by Jane Burton and Kim Taylor
Published by Dorling Kindersley, Inc.

An Extraordinary Egg
by Leo Lionni
Published by Alfred A. Knopf, Inc.

Follow the Moon
By Sarah Weeks
Illustrated by Suzanne Duranceau
Published by HarperCollins Publishers

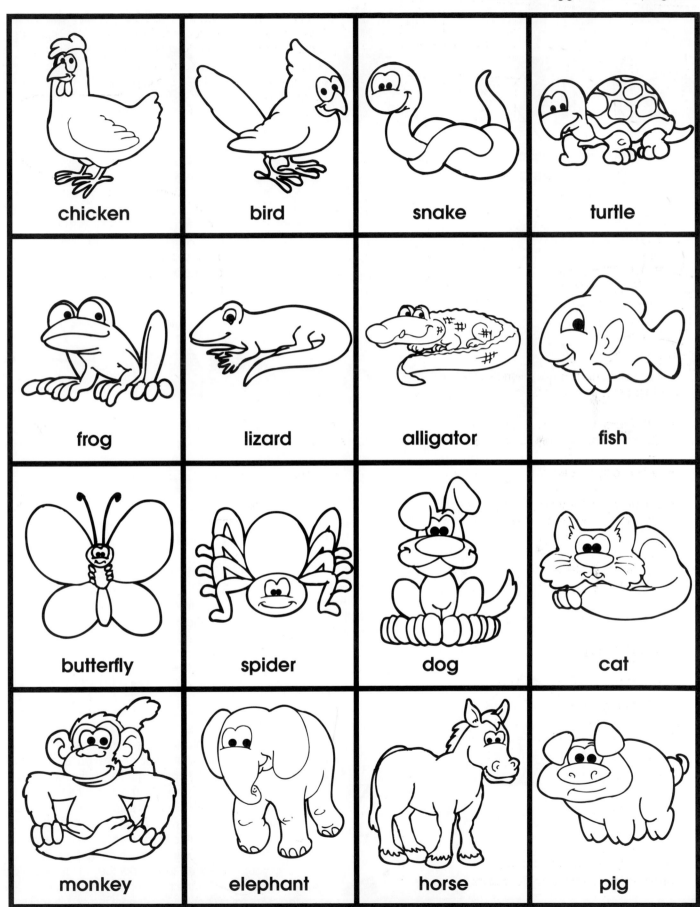

chicken   bird   snake   turtle

frog   lizard   alligator   fish

butterfly   spider   dog   cat

monkey   elephant   horse   pig

A Flurry of Flowers

Pick a bouquet of these flower-related ideas to bring your youngsters' learning into full bloom.

ideas by Katie Padilla

Flannelboard Flowers

Invite youngsters to practice their counting skills with this flower-filled song. To begin, copy the stem pattern (page 27) ten times on green construction paper and the flower pattern (page 27) five times each on two different colors of construction paper. Then cut out all the patterns. Glue each flower to a stem, laminate the completed flowers, and prepare them for flannelboard use. To use, have student volunteers display the corresponding number of flowers on the flannelboard as they sing this song. After several rounds, extend this idea by challenging students to create a color pattern as they count the flowers.

Ten Little Flowers
(sung to the tune of "Ten Little Indians")

One little, two little, three little flowers.
Four little, five little, six little flowers.
Seven little, eight little, nine little flowers.
Ten little flowers in bloom!

Flower March

Counting skills will blossom with this flowery movement game! Enlarge the flower pattern on page 27; then make a class set plus a few extras on assorted colors of construction paper. Laminate and cut out each flower. Then use a wipe-off pen to label each flower with a numeral from 1 to 10. Tape the cutouts on the floor to create a large circle. To play, instruct students to march around the flowers while you play music. When you stop the music, have each child stand next to the flower closest to her. Then call out an action, such as "hop on one foot," "clap your hands," or "touch your toes." Have each child perform the action the number of times corresponding to the numeral on her flower. Repeat the activity, calling out a different action for each round of play. Continue as long as student interest *and* energy dictate.

The Flower Shop

If you're looking for a special arrangement that includes listening, counting, color, and personal information skills, this floral shop is sure to deliver! Collect a large assortment of artificial flowers: silk, plastic, and student made. Put them in your housekeeping center along with bud vases, planters, ribbon, sheets of cellophane, play money, a toy cash register, two play phones, and a shop sign. Then invite small groups to visit the center. Appoint two students to be shop attendants. Assign one to prepare flower arrangements for walk-in customers and the other to prepare phone orders and to make deliveries. Encourage the other students—the customers—to place their flower orders in person or by phone. Instruct the call-in customers to give their addresses to assure proper delivery. After each order is filled and purchased, reassign roles so that each child has the opportunity to be a shop attendant and a customer. Then have youngsters prepare the shop for the next group.

Not *Just* for *Flower!*

Use this idea to help youngsters discover that words beginning with F are all around them. To begin, write a class-generated list of words that start with F on chart paper. Then have each child cut out a large construction paper flower and stem and leaves. Instruct him to glue the pieces together; then help him label the front of his flower with "F is for *flower* and…" On the back of his flower, have the child glue magazine cutouts (or draw pictures) of things whose names begin with F. Then invite each child to share his work with the class. Later, encourage him to take his project home to show his family how his knowledge of F is flourishing!

Flowers With Flavor

Flowers and food make a fantastic combination in this tasty idea! To make a placemat for this activity, ask each child to decorate a 9" x 12" sheet of construction paper with four flower stems. Help children label their papers; then laminate all the mats. At snacktime, give each child his placemat and four flower-shaped cookies (such as scallop-edged butter cookies). Have him spread peanut butter on each cookie and then place an M&M's® candy in the center of each one. Instruct the child to place each cookie flower on a stem. Then encourage him to count his flowers and to name the color of each flower center before he eats his floral treat. Afterward, have each child clean his mat; then invite him to use wipe-off markers to draw a flower on each stem and additional flowers and details on his picture.

Floral Greeting Cards

Invite each child to express her feelings for someone special with a card that flowers with affection. First, make a class supply of the text box on page 27. Then have each child fold a colorful sheet of 9" x 12" construction paper in half. Next, ask her to cut out a supply of flower pictures from magazines, calendars, wallpaper samples, or gift wrap. Then have her glue the pictures onto the front of her card. When the glue is dry, have the child cut out and glue the text box to the inside of her card. Then help her write someone's name on the line. Invite her to sign her card and to draw a border around the text as she desires. Finally, encourage each child to deliver her card to her special loved one.

A Flower for the Fridge

This fanciful flower magnet makes a perfect home-school phonics connection. To make tracers for the magnet, cut out several tagboard copies of the flower and stem patterns on page 27. Then have each child trace a stem onto green craft foam and a flower onto another color of craft foam. Help him cut out the pieces; then have him use craft glue to glue them together. Invite each child to decorate his flower with supplies such as permanent markers, wiggle eyes, and craft foam scraps. Attach a piece of magnetic tape to the back of each flower. Then send each child home with his magnet and a note requesting that parents display the flower on the refrigerator. Explain that the flower is meant to serve as a reminder to reinforce words that begin with *F* as they occur. What a fantastic way to reinforce phonics with the family!

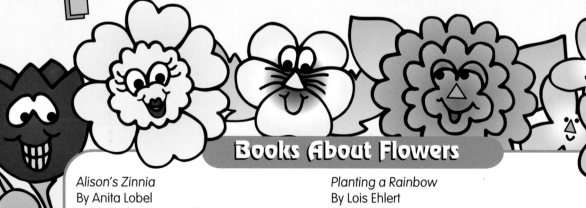

Books About Flowers

Alison's Zinnia
By Anita Lobel
Published by Greenwillow Books

Flower Garden
By Eve Bunting
Illustrated by Kathryn Hewitt
Published by Harcourt Brace & Company

Planting a Rainbow
By Lois Ehlert
Published by Harcourt Brace Jovanovich, Publishers

Sunflower
By Miela Ford
Illustrated by Sally Noll
Published by Greenwillow Books

Patterns

Use with "Flannelboard Flowers" on page 24 and "A Flower for the Fridge" on page 26.
Use the flower pattern with "Flower March" on page 24.

flower

stem

Text Box

Use with "Floral Greeting Cards" on page 26.

Dear _____,

I filled this card with flowers for you,
Lots of love, and good wishes, too!

From,

Let's Get Groceries

This cartload of grocery-related activities is filled with bargains for learning. Check it out!

ideas by Diane Gilliam

Guessing Groceries

Bring a bit of the grocery store into your classroom with a guessing game that reinforces counting and comparing sets. To prepare, fill one or more grocery bags with items (or empty containers) that are commonly purchased at a grocery store. Then cut open and flatten a large, brown paper bag to use as chart paper. Label the chart "What's in the Bag?" During group time, tell youngsters that each bag is filled with things from the grocery store. Then challenge them to guess what's in the bag(s), giving clues if necessary. Write their responses on the chart. Afterward, invite one child at a time to remove an item from the bag. Help him search the list for the name of the item. If it is on the chart, have the child check it off. Once all of the items are removed, count them together. Then compare the results to the number of correct guesses on the chart.

A-Shopping We Will Go

Once your youngsters have had a sampling of grocery store fare (in "Guessing Groceries"), arrange a class visit to the real thing. To prepare, make several copies of the checklist on page 31. When you arrive at the store, give one checklist and a pencil to each small group (and chaperone). Instruct the groups to look for each item on the list as they tour the store. When an item is found, have a child check it off. At the end of your visit, invite groups to review and compare their lists. Did everybody find everything? Was the searching hard or easy? What grocery-finding tips did they discover?

Thanks a Bunch!

After your grocery store visit, help students create this class thank-you letter to send to your grocery store host(s). To begin, cut open and flatten a large paper bag. Then write a class-generated message on the bag. To decorate the note, have each child cut out a grocery-related picture from a magazine and glue it to the border of the bag. Then have each child sign his name near his cutout. Ready for delivery!

The Job Market

While at the grocery store, your class most likely observed several different types of employees at work. Use this activity to explore the different jobs of grocery store workers. Cut open and flatten a large paper bag to use as a chart. Title the chart "Jobs at the Grocery Store." Then invite students to list the titles and tasks of each grocery store worker that they recall. Write their responses on the chart. After discussing the roles of each worker, display the chart in your dramatic-play center as a reference for "A Classy Grocery Store."

Jobs at the Grocery Store

Cashier	Bagger	Butcher	Baker	Deli Worker	Stock Clerk
scans groceries	puts groceries in bags	cuts meat	bakes cakes, cupcakes, doughnuts, bagels, cookies	slices meat and cheese	puts food and stuff on shelves
takes money	pushes cart to car	wraps meat up to sell		makes sandwiches	
	loads groceries into car			makes potato salad and chicken salad	

A Classy Grocery Store

Extend your youngsters' learning opportunities with this classroom grocery store. In advance, ask parents to send in clean, empty food packages. (To make cardboard packages more durable, stuff them with newspaper; then tape the ends.) Arrange the packages and additional supplies, such as toy foods, play money, wallets, a toy cash register, grocery bags, handled baskets, coupons, grocery store flyers, paper, and pencils. When the store is ready for business, invite small groups to visit the center. Encourage students to take turns role-playing shoppers, as well as grocery store workers (refer to the chart from "The Job Market" for ideas). At the end of each group's visit, have youngsters prepare the store for the next group.

Grocery Riddles

Share some of these grocery-related brain teasers to inspire thinking. If desired, show a sample or picture of each item after students identify it from the clues. Later, invite volunteers to secretly select items from your class grocery store and then make up their own riddles to share with the group.

- I am dry and crunchy. You pour milk over me. *(cereal)*
- I come in a plastic bag. I'm usually sliced. You might spread peanut butter and jelly on me. *(bread)*
- I am shaped like a tube. I am often cooked on a grill and then put into a bun. People like to dress me with ketchup and mustard—sometimes even sauerkraut! *(hot dog)*
- I am round and sweet, and I have a hole in my middle. *(doughnut)*
- I might come in a powder or a liquid form. You put me in a machine, and I clean your clothes. *(laundry detergent)*

I come in a plastic bag. I'm usually sliced. You might spread peanut butter and jelly on me.

Mystery Groceries

Promote language and thinking skills with these mystery bags of groceries. To begin, give each child four blank notecards. Ask him to glue a cutout or a drawing of a different grocery item on each card. Help each child label his cards, write his name on a small paper bag and on the backs of his cards, and then put the cards in his bag. Then divide your class into groups of three or four. Invite each child, in turn, to describe a picture in his bag without showing it. Encourage him to continue to give clues. Whoever guesses correctly gets the card. Continue until all the groceries have been guessed. Afterward, return the groceries to the original owners. Then invite each child to take his bag home and play this game with his family.

Dear Parent,
We are learning about solids and liquids that can be purchased at a grocery store. Please explore your kitchen with your child to find examples of solid foods and liquid foods. Then write the name of each item in the corresponding column. Return the completed form to school by

_____. Thank you!
(date)

_____
(teacher)

Solid Foods   **Liquid Foods**

Name _____

A Matter of Groceries

Strengthen the connection between home, school, and community with this grocery-related science activity. To prepare, copy the recording form on page 31 for each student. Then gather a few solid foods and a few liquid foods. Tell youngsters that most of the edible items in a grocery store are either *solids* or *liquids*. Show them each group of items and then ask them to compare and contrast the groups. Pour each liquid into a different container to demonstrate how it takes on the shape of the container it is in. Then guide students to state that solids keep their own shapes while liquids do not. Afterward, send each child home with the recording form to explore the food in her own home. When each child returns her completed form, invite her to share her findings with the class. To further reinforce the differences between solids and liquids, encourage youngsters to classify their lunch or snack items.

Grocery Math

Pack in opportunities to practice math skills with these grocery-related center activities. To prepare, put one basket of each of the following in your math center: various sizes of canned goods, assorted boxed items, and various sizes of plastic bottles. Then invite student pairs to visit the center to do one or more of the following activities:

- Sequence the items from one basket by size.
- Use the contents of the baskets to create a pattern. Explain the pattern to your partner.
- Count the items in each basket. Which basket has the most items?
- Use a balance to weigh and compare the weights.

A-Shopping We Will Go

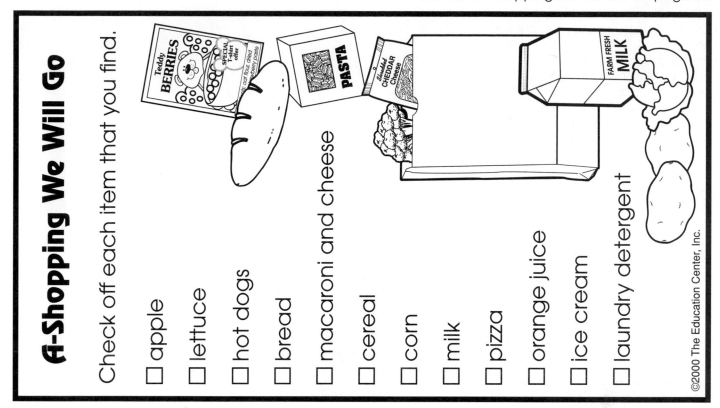

Check off each item that you find.

☐ apple
☐ lettuce
☐ hot dogs
☐ bread
☐ macaroni and cheese
☐ cereal
☐ corn
☐ milk
☐ pizza
☐ orange juice
☐ ice cream
☐ laundry detergent

©2000 The Education Center, Inc.

Dear Parent,
We are learning about solids and liquids that can be purchased at a grocery store. Please explore your kitchen with your child to find examples of solid foods and liquid foods. Then write the name of each item in the corresponding column. Return the completed form to school by _____. Thank you!

_____
(date)

_____
(teacher)

Solid Foods   **Liquid Foods**

Name _____

©2000 The Education Center, Inc.

Hand It Over!

Here's a handful of ideas to get little fingers involved in lots of fun and learning!

ideas by Suzanne Moore

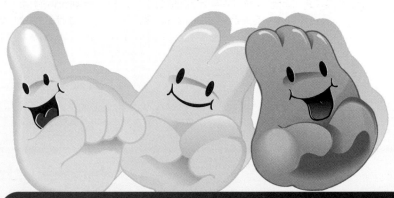

Busy Hands

How much can those little hands do? Find out with this lively little song! Encourage students to create motions to go along with the song. Then be sure to give your youngsters a big *hand* after their performance!

Busy Hands
(adapted to the tune of "Six Little Ducks")

There are lots of things that my hands can do.
I can wiggle my fingers. I can squeeze the glue.
I can write my name and tap my knee.
I can use my fingers to count one, two, three.
One, two, three.
I can use my fingers to count one, two, three.

There are lots of things that my hands can do.
I can button my shirt. I can tie my shoe.
I can brush my teeth, wash my hair with shampoo.
I can use my hands to cover my "a-choo!"
Cover my "a-choo!"
I can use my hands to cover my "a-choo!"

There are lots of things that my hands can do.
I can build with blocks. I can hold a big balloon.
I can flap my wings like a bird in the sky.
I can clap my hands and wave good-bye.
Wave good-bye.
I can clap my hands and wave good-bye!

My Hands Can...

All hands are needed to make this fun class book in which hands are the main attraction! To prepare, you'll need a class supply of large sheets of white construction paper, two colorful construction paper covers, and several colorful hand cutouts. First, glue the hand cutouts to the front cover. Then fold each white sheet so that one inch remains uncovered on the left side (as shown). Next, have each child trace his hands with his wrists placed on the folded side of the construction paper (see the illustration). Encourage each child to color his tracings to match his skin tone. Then help him write "[Josh]'s hands can..." on that page. Next, have each child open the flap and draw several things that he can do with his hands. Record each child's dictation near the corresponding picture. To assemble the book, stack the pages with the fold to the right, and staple them along the left side between the covers. This handmade book will be a handy class favorite!

Note: If desired, introduce the activity above by sharing a book about hands, such as *Hands, Hands, Hands* by Marcia Vaughan (MONDO Publishing).

Sherri

Dem Bones

No bones about it—there are *lots* of bones in one little hand! Your little ones will delight in creating these imitation X rays of their own hands. In advance, ask a local hospital to donate old hand X rays. For each student, cut white straws in a variety of lengths. (Two-inch, one-inch, and ¹/₂-inch pieces work well.) During circle time, show the X rays to your students. Lead students to conclude that one hand has lots of bones inside it. At a center, have each child use a white crayon to trace around her hand on black construction paper. Then, using craft glue, she arranges and glues straw pieces to the hand to resemble bones. Hey! They look like X rays!

Little Hands, Big Hands

Strengthen the home-school connection with this math-related project. For each child, duplicate the parent letter on page 35 and staple it to a folded 12" x 18" sheet of colorful construction paper. (For larger families, send home several sheets of paper.) Instruct each child to trace each family member's hand on the construction paper. Have him print his own name on each tracing then cut it out. Ask each child to bring his collection of hand cutouts back to school. During small-group time, have each child find the littlest hand in his collection. Then have him find the biggest hand. Next, have each child glue his family's hands in order, from the smallest to the largest, on a wide tagboard strip. Using various classroom items (such as paper clips, erasers, and crayons), have each student measure the hands from the longest finger to the wrist. Assist each child in recording the measurements on his project. Busy little hands!

David

David

David

left	right
	Ben
Eva	Eric
Resa	Sophie
Josh	Carlos

Left or Right?

Each student lends a hand in this small-group graphing activity. In advance, make a two-column graph. Label one column "left" and the other one "right." Begin the activity by asking questions such as these: Which hand do you use to color? Which hand do you use to hold a fork? Which hand do you use to throw a ball? Encourage each student to respond to each question by raising the hand she uses for that particular activity. Then explain the idea of *hand dominance*. Ask the questions again, encouraging each child to notice which hand she raises more often. Next, have each student trace her dominant hand onto a colorful sheet of construction paper and cut it out. Print each child's name on her hand cutout. Then help each child tape her hand cutout to the appropriate side of the graph. What handy ideas does this graph reveal?

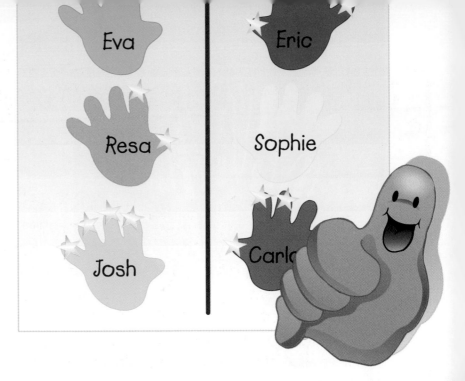

Helping Hands

Reinforce positive behavior in your classroom with these helping hand certificates! In advance, make a class supply of the certificate on page 35. Then, when you'd like to recognize a child for lending a helping hand, put a star sticker on one finger of her hand cutout (see "Left or Right?" on page 33). When a child has a star on each finger, fill in a certificate for her; then hand it over with all the appropriate fanfare. Handy dandy!

Handmade Treats

A handful of fun is in store as your crew creates these tasty little snacks! In advance, prepare your favorite gingerbread cookie dough. Also cut out a few tagboard hand tracers. Have each child use a permanent marker to trace a hand tracer on a sheet of waxed paper. Have him write his name next to the traced hand and then flip the waxed paper over. Instruct each child to roll a small portion of dough between his hands (to make a finger) and then press the dough onto his hand outline. Have him repeat the process until all five fingers are completed. Then have him press additional dough into the palm area. Encourage students to decorate their dough hands with icing, chocolate chips, sprinkles, and raisins. Bake according to your recipe's directions. In the hands of your students, these tempting treats won't last long!

Grab a Handful of These Books!

Hands!
Written by Virginia L. Kroll
Published by Boyds Mills
   Press

Hand Rhymes
Collected by Marc Brown
Published by Dutton
   Children's Books

The Handmade Alphabet
Written by Laura Rankin
Published by Puffin Pied
   Piper Books

Touching
Written by Henry Pluckrose
Published by Gareth
   Stevens Publishing

Dear Parent,

Our class is learning all sorts of interesting things about hands! As you and your child go about your normal routines, please try to talk about how you both use your hands. Then help your child trace each family member's hand on the attached sheet of construction paper, print your child's name on the tracing, and then cut it out. Place the cutouts in an envelope or resealable plastic bag; then have your child bring them back to school by _____. We'll use the handy cutouts as we explore math skills! Thank you for supporting your child's learning!

Sincerely,

Hands Up

for

_____!

Thanks for your
"handy-dandy" help!
Congratulations!

Icky Stuff!

Youngsters will be up to their elbows in learning fun with these icky, ooey-gooey ideas!

ideas by Suzanne Moore

All Things Icky

Begin your icky investigation with a fingerplay that will have your youngsters squirming with delight! After reciting the last line, invite students to name their favorite icky things and record their responses on chart paper.

Gooey slime, a glowing worm.
Icky things just make me squirm!
Oozing mud and squiggly snakes.
Icky things give me the shakes!
Icky slime and icky bugs,
Icky goo and icky slugs,
Icky mud and all the rest.
What icky things do you like best?

Wiggle fingers slowly.
Wiggle fingers faster and squirm all over.
Wiggle arms slowly.
Wiggle arms faster and knock knees.
Slowly crawl hand up opposite arm.
Slowly crawl other hand up opposite arm.
Rub hands together.
Point to a friend.

Why Is It Icky?

Bugs, slime, worms, goo. What things are icky and why? Display the list of icky things made in "All Things Icky." Then encourage a discussion by having each child tell why he thinks the item he named is icky. Add these responses to your list. To pack this idea with curriculum punch, have your kindergartners classify each listed item as a living or nonliving thing. Review the list and have children take turns circling living things with a green marker and nonliving things with a brown marker. Display this list for little ones to review throughout your icky study. Perhaps it would make a good read-the-room activity…if it's not too icky!

snakes—They are creepy. Jenna
spiders—Just too spidery. Cole
slugs—Just gross. Kelly
oatmeal—It's lumpy but it's good for you. Claire
spider webs—They're invisible. Joe
green junk at the lake—It is slippery and squishy. Seth

Mud Pie Magic

Oh, boy! Ooey-gooey mud! Youngsters will be eager to plunge into this mud exploration center that encourages small-muscle development. To set up this center, fill your sand table or a large plastic tub with soil; then add just enough water to make a thick mud mixture. (For added fun, hide a few rubber worms in the mud!) Next, provide some pie pans, spoons, and measuring cups at the center. Then encourage your little ones to visit the center and make some homemade mud pies. If desired, provide thin plastic gloves for youngsters who are squeamish about squishing around. For easy cleanup, provide a water-filled plastic bucket and paper towels near the center.

Yikes, Snakes!

Slithery snakes make some people squirm. But not Ali, the main character in Angela Johnson's book *The Girl Who Wore Snakes* (Orchard Books). She wears her pet snakes everywhere! After reading this story to your class, make several of these unique necktie snakes for your students to take turns wearing. In advance, visit your local thrift store in search of several colorful neckties. To transform a tie into a snake, tie a knot at the narrow end of the tie. Stuff the tie with fiberfill, stopping about five inches from the open, wide end of the tie. Sew a seam across the opening; then fold over the remaining fabric to form the snake's head. Hot-glue the folded fabric in place. When the glue is dry, sew button eyes and a ribbon tongue to the snake's head. Place these "tie-rific" creeping critters in your dramatic-play area and invite your youngsters to wear the snakes and retell the story.

It's Slime Time!

Science concepts flow naturally out of this slimy small-group activity. In preparation for this messy—but fun—activity, cover your workspace. Then follow the recipe below to make one batch of slime. Give each child a small portion of the slime on a waxed paper workmat. Direct her to place the waxed paper on a hard surface and pound the slime with her fist. (It will feel hard and solid.) Then have her pick up the slime and hold it in the palms of her hands. (It will ooze through her fingers like a liquid.) Encourage students to explore this unusual substance and invite them to describe the experience.

Slime

Materials needed:
one 16-oz. box of cornstarch
green food coloring
1 1/2 c. water

Pour the box of cornstarch into a large bowl; then use food coloring to tint 1 1/2 cups of water dark green. Slowly stir the water into the cornstarch and mix to an even consistency. It should run through your fingers when held gently, but feel solid if you slap the mixture. Adjust the amounts of water and cornstarch until you achieve the right consistency.

Do Bugs Bug You?

If you ask people their opinion of bugs, most likely these critters are high on their icky lists. Your youngsters, however, are sure to be thrilled with Margery Facklam's *The Big Bug Book* (Little, Brown and Company). After showing students the pictures and paraphrasing the text, invite youngsters to create their own imaginary icky bugs. Stock your art center with pipe cleaners, round-tipped toothpicks, wiggle eyes, and a class supply of small Styrofoam® balls. Have each child visit the center and create a bug by sticking pipe cleaners and toothpicks into a Styrofoam ball. Then have her glue on wiggle eyes and other miscellaneous craft items. Hang these completed creatures around your room, but be prepared for visitors to shriek, "Eeek!"

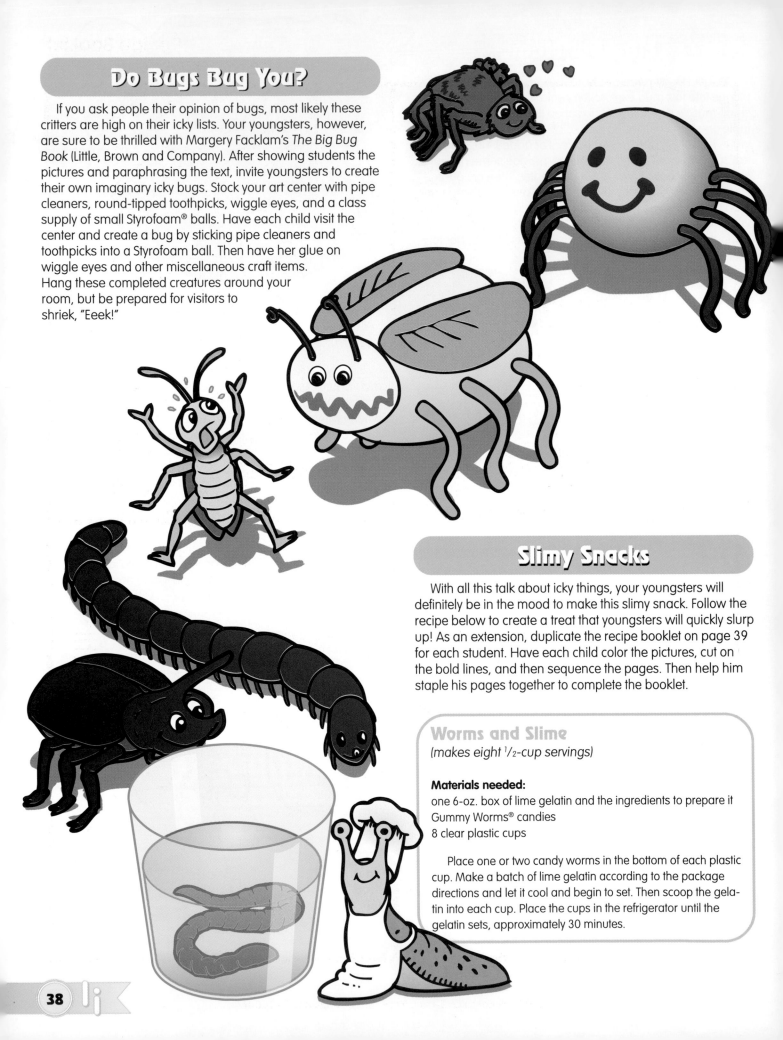

Slimy Snacks

With all this talk about icky things, your youngsters will definitely be in the mood to make this slimy snack. Follow the recipe below to create a treat that youngsters will quickly slurp up! As an extension, duplicate the recipe booklet on page 39 for each student. Have each child color the pictures, cut on the bold lines, and then sequence the pages. Then help him staple his pages together to complete the booklet.

Worms and Slime
(makes eight ¹/₂-cup servings)

Materials needed:
one 6-oz. box of lime gelatin and the ingredients to prepare it
Gummy Worms® candies
8 clear plastic cups

Place one or two candy worms in the bottom of each plastic cup. Make a batch of lime gelatin according to the package directions and let it cool and begin to set. Then scoop the gelatin into each cup. Place the cups in the refrigerator until the gelatin sets, approximately 30 minutes.

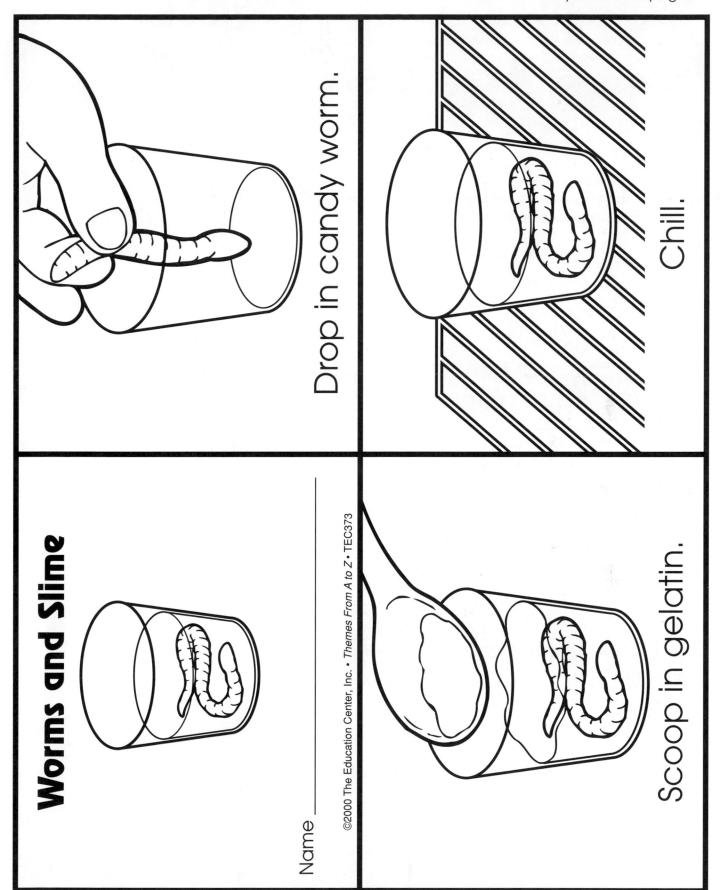

Drop in candy worm.

Chill.

Worms and Slime

Name

©2000 The Education Center, Inc. • *Themes From A to Z* • TEC373

Scoop in gelatin.

Jam-and-Jelly Jamboree

Jumpin' jelly jars! It's time for jam-and-jelly activities! Your youngsters will be tasting sweet success as they explore these sweet treats.

ideas by Chrissy Yuhouse and Sherri Lynn Kuntz

Jam
thicker
sticky
smells good
I see fruit.
sweet
has seeds

Jelly
runny
sticky
smells good
slimy
sweet
no seeds

Jam or Jelly?

Jump-start your little ones' critical-thinking skills by having them compare jam to jelly. Place a bowl of jam on one side of a table and a bowl of jelly on the other side. Also provide paper plates, plastic knives, and crackers. Have each child look, touch, taste, and smell to compare the two choices. Record student responses on labeled jar-shaped cutouts. So what's the same? What's different?

Sweet Attractions

This sticky science experiment is sure to attract your students' attention, as well as that of some other little critters! In advance, gather a class supply of small paper plates, cocktail bread slices, and plastic knives. Also provide a jar of jelly or jam. To begin, have each child spread a little jelly or jam on a slice of bread and place it on a plate. Then lead your children outside to position their plates on the ground. (If possible, place the plates near a window for easy observation.) Encourage students to make predictions about what might happen. Then have students check periodically to see what *is* happening. Encourage each child to record his observations in a science journal.

A Giant Jam Sandwich

Inspired by *The Giant Jam Sandwich* by John Vernon Lord (Houghton Mifflin), a hands-on giant jam sandwich is just the thing for your dramatic-play area! In advance, visit your local craft store to purchase thick foam pieces and large pieces of jam-colored felt. Trim the foam to resemble bread slices and the felt to look like jam. Put the giant sandwich ingredients in your dramatic-play center along with toy trucks and toy bees or bugs. After sharing the story with your class, encourage children who visit this center to act out their own original giant jam sandwich stories!

Jelly Painting

Jazz up your paint center with this hands-on art activity! In a center, arrange a variety of jelly flavors and a class supply of poster board sheets. Put a spoon in each flavor of jelly. Then invite each child to fingerpaint a picture with the jelly. After the paintings dry, display these unique jelly creations!

Which Flavor Do You Favor?

What do you get when you mix math with jam and jelly? A tantalizing taste-testing activity! To prepare, you'll need a small jar of each of the following: mint jelly, orange marmalade, grape jam, and strawberry jam. Also provide a serving spoon for each jar, a class supply of small paper plates, and four crackers per child. Duplicate the graph on page 43 to make a class supply. (If you need longer columns in your graph, simply copy the graph again. Then cut and paste to extend the columns as needed.) To begin the activity, have each child spoon a sample of each of the jelly and jam flavors onto a different cracker. Invite each child to taste each sample to determine her favorite. In turn, ask each child to announce her favorite flavor. As she announces it, instruct all the children to color in a box in the corresponding column of their charts. (For younger children, enlarge the chart and use that copy to make a class graph.) Continue until each child has had a turn to announce her favorite flavor. Then discuss what the graphs reveal.

Jam Jingle

Prepare your youngsters for a squishy, squashy jam-making session by jamming to the following song! Encourage your students to make up actions as they sing.

Jam Jingle
(sung to the tune of "She'll Be Comin' Round the Mountain")

We'll be making our own jam in school today. (Yippee!)
We'll be making our own jam in school today. (Yippee!)
We'll be making our own jam. We'll be making our own jam.
We'll be making our own jam in school today. (Yippee!)

We'll be squishin' all the fruit that's in the bag. (Squish, squash!)
We'll be squishin' all the fruit that's in the bag. (Squish, squash!)
We'll be squishin' all the fruit. We'll be squishin' all the fruit.
We'll be squishin' all the fruit that's in the bag. (Squish, squash!)

It will taste so very good when it is done. (Yum-yum!)
It will taste so very good when it is done. (Yum-yum!)
It will taste so very good. It will taste so very good.
It will taste so very good when it is done. (Yum-yum!)

Jam in a Jiffy

Mmmmm-mmmm, this jam-making activity will get your little ones joining together to make a class supply of homemade strawberry jam. In advance, have parents donate the ingredients for your favorite no-cook strawberry jam. (Most boxes of liquid fruit pectin include recipes.) When all the ingredients have arrived, have students help you put the ingredients into a large resealable bag. Seal the bag, letting out most of the air, and then seat it inside another bag to guard against leaks. (If desired, prepare more than one batch of ingredients at a time and have children work in small groups.) Ask each child to take a turn squishing, squeezing, and squashing the ingredients together. (If desired, sing "Jam Jingle" as children work.) Follow the recipe directions for letting the mixture set; then refrigerate. At snacktime, serve this sweet treat on crackers. A syrupy jam is great on top of ice cream or pancakes!

Jam-and-Jelly Books

Bread and Jam for Frances
Written by Russell Hoban
Published by HarperCollins
    Children's Books, 1993

Jamberry
Written by Bruce Degen
Published by Harperfestival, 1975

Peanut Butter & Jelly for Shabbos
Written by Dina Rosenfeld
Published by Hachai Publishing, 1995

Peanut Butter and Jelly:
    A Play Rhyme
Illustrated by Nadine Bernard
    Westcott
Published by E. P. Dutton, 1992

Check your local library for
the following:

Jam: A True Story
Written by Margaret Mahy

Mint Jelly	Orange Marmalade	Grape Jam	Strawberry Jam

Here Come the Kittens!

Don't "paws" another moment! Use these cross-curricular kitten ideas to give your youngsters the "purr-fect" combination of learning and fun!

ideas by Chrissy Yuhouse

Kittens live on farms or in houses.
Aaron

I think kittens like to eat meat.
Athena

Kitties play with balls and yarn.
Bryan

Kittens meow and sometimes purr.
Sean

I believe they live all over the world!
And in the wild.
Dakota

They are fluffy.
Sherri

Cats look alike. They have pointy ears and long, long tails.
Rick

Calling All Kittens!

Get your little ones chatting about kittens with this unique circle-time activity that gives you some valuable assessment information! In advance, gather a bell and two play phones. To begin the activity, keep one of the phones for yourself and have children start passing the other one around the circle. When you ring the bell, ask the child who is holding the phone at that moment to "answer" it. Ask that child to share what he already knows about kittens or what he would like to know. Record the student's response on chart paper. Continue in this manner until each child has had a chance to share. Follow up by displaying the chart so children can "call" on it throughout the unit!

Kitten Chorus

Youngsters will get all wrapped up in this song about kitten activities! As you sing the song below with your children, encourage them to act it out. Repeat the song again, having youngsters replace the underlined word with a new action word each time.

Kitten Chorus
(sung to the tune of "Up on the Housetop")

What do kittens like to do?
They like to [climb]! That's what they do.
Wiggle a feather and watch the fun.
A cute little kitten on the run!

Purr, purr, purr—pounce and play,
Purr, purr, purr—fun all day!
Wiggle a feather and watch the fun.
A cute little kitten on the run!

Kitten Kibble

Who's hungry? This kid version of kitten kibble will have your youngsters meowing for more!

You will need:
1 large resealable plastic bag
1 c. white chocolate chips
$\frac{1}{2}$ c. peanut butter
$\frac{1}{4}$ c. butter
1 tsp. vanilla
$1\frac{1}{2}$ c. each of three different kinds of Goldfish® crackers
$1\frac{1}{2}$ c. powdered sugar

Using a microwave, melt the white chocolate chips, peanut butter, and butter. Stir in the vanilla and the Goldfish crackers. Pour the mixture into a large resealable plastic bag and then gently squeeze the bag until thoroughly mixed. Lastly, add the powdered sugar and shake the bag until all the crackers are coated.

Colorful Kittens

Students will sink their paws into this colorful, personalized project! To make a kitten's body, help a child paint her hand with her choice of tempera paint. Then have her press her hand onto a piece of paper to make a print. Invite her to repeat the process to make as many prints (kittens) as she likes. Let the paint dry. Next, have her use crayons or markers to add kitten features and other details. If desired, provide teardrop-shaped sponges for sponge-painting mice on the pictures!

Kitten Counters

Pounce on math concepts with these little kitten counters! Make 11 copies of page 47. Color the patterns if desired; then laminate the pages and cut out the patterns. Next, print a different numeral from 0 to 10 on each mother cat. Place the cats and kittens in a basket in a center. Invite children to match the correct number of kittens to each of the labeled mother cats.

A gray kitten? A striped kitten? How about a tortoise shell kitten? Invite your students to explore the many kinds of kittens and cats and their variety of colors! Begin by sharing *Kittens: An Ideal Introduction to the World of Kittens* by Carey Scott (Dorling Kindersley Ltd.). Then guide a discussion about fur colors and kitten-related vocabulary. Afterward, use this new vocabulary when you chant the verse below. Each time you repeat the verse, ask children to replace the underlined word with another word, such as *tabby, long-haired, Persian, Siamese, white, black,* etc.

Little [calico] kitty,
So very soft and pretty.
Little [calico] kitty,
I wish that you were mine!

Fish in the Dish

Hmmm, something's fishy around here! Can you sniff out just what or *who* it is? In advance, find a stuffed or toy fish (or use a construction paper cutout). Place the fish in a dish in the middle of a circle of seated children. To play the game, choose one child to be the kitten. Have him turn around and cover his eyes. Then silently select another child to take the fish and hide it somewhere on herself. Have the kitten turn around while the class chants "Kitty, kitty, where's your fish? Somebody took it from your dish!" Encourage the kitten to crawl around the circle and "meow" to guess who took his fish. When the keeper of the fish is identified, she becomes the kitten and play begins again. Play until everyone has had a turn to be the kitten. Meow!

"Paws-atively" Playful!

Here's the "purr-fect" kitten costume for dramatic play!
Headband: Twist three long pipe cleaners (whiskers) together in the middle. Tape the middle of the whiskers onto one end of a four-inch strip of poster board. To complete the nose piece, glue a pink construction paper nose on top of the whiskers. Attach the free end of the nosepiece to a tagboard headband. Then attach two construction paper ears.

Paws: To make a front paw, punch two holes in a large paw cutout. Insert a long pipe cleaner through the holes to make a bracelet. Make each back paw the same way, but use a shorter length of pipe cleaner so a child can wrap it around his shoelaces or straps.

Collar: Decorate a loose-fitting tagboard collar with a nametag, bell, beads, and craft jewels. Fasten the collar together with pipe cleaner pieces.

Kitten Tales

The Dog Who Had Kittens
Written by Polly Robertus
Published by Holiday House, Inc.

Five Little Kittens
Written by Nancy Jewell
Published by Houghton Mifflin Company

Three Little Kittens
Written by Paul Galdone
Published by Houghton Mifflin Company

Where's My Kitten? A Lift-the-Flap Book
Written by Michele Coxon
Published by Puffin Books

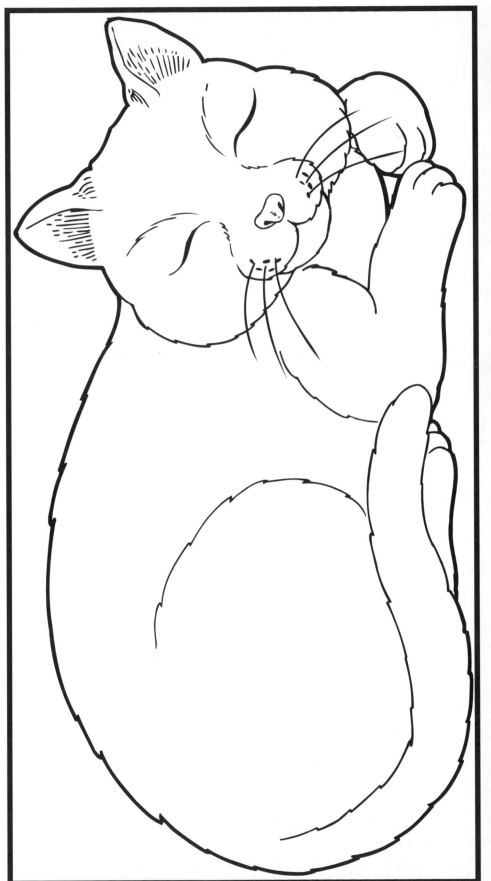

Lots of Lemons and Limes

This lively lemon-and-lime unit will add zest to any early childhood classroom. From crafts to recipes to science explorations, the following ideas and activities are simply sub*lime*!

ideas by Michele Dare

Freshly Squeezed

Splash into this unit with a lemonade and limeade taste test. Follow the recipe below to make a batch of lemonade and a batch of limeade. Have students sample both drinks and then describe each one. Record their responses on lemon- and lime-shaped cutouts. Display the charts in your room and refer to them again during "Which 'ade Gets the Grade?" (below).

Refreshing Lemonade
(makes approximately 64 ounces)

$1^1/_2$ c. freshly squeezed lemon juice (6 lemons)
6 c. water
$1^1/_4$ c. sugar
ice

Mix the juice, water, and sugar together in a pitcher. Stir until the sugar dissolves. Add ice and serve.

To make limeade, substitute $1^1/_2$ cups of lime juice (eight limes) for the lemon juice.

Which 'ade Gets the Grade?

This graphing activity is best when served shortly after your taste test! On a large sheet of paper, draw two identical drinking glasses. Cut equally sized yellow and green construction paper strips that are the same width as the glasses. Review students' responses to the taste test in "Freshly Squeezed"; then have each child decide which drink she prefers. If she prefers lemonade, give her a yellow strip for the lemonade graph. If limeade is her choice, give her a green strip for the limeade graph. Direct her to write her name on the strip and then tape it on the appropriate graph. When the graphs are complete, discuss what they reveal.

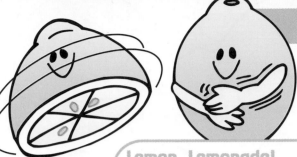

Lemonade Serenade

Since your youngsters will be inspired by their own lemonade and limeade making, it won't be hard to squeeze some singing out of them! Here's a fun interactive song that just might work up a thirst for *more* lemonade! (For a corresponding booklet idea, see "Read All About It!" below.)

Lemon, Lemonade!
(sung to the tune of "Peanut, Peanut Butter")

First you take the lemons and you cut 'em.
You cut 'em.
Then you take the lemons and you squeeze 'em.
You squeeze 'em.
Then you add the sugar and the water,
The water.
Then you drop in ice cubes and you stir it.
You stir it.
Pour yourself a glass and you drink it.
You drink it.
Lemon, lemonade—yeah!
Lemon, lemonade—yeah!

Act out holding lemon on cutting board and slicing it.

Act out juicing a lemon.

Pretend to pour using right hand, then left hand.

Pretend to drop in ice cubes and make stirring motion.

Pretend to pour and drink.

Throw hands up in the air when singing "yeah!"

Yeah!

Read All About It!

Lemonade and literacy—what a pair! After learning the song "Lemon, Lemonade!" (above), your little ones will be eager to make and read this corresponding booklet. To make one, duplicate the text strips on page 52 and the booklet cover on page 53. Cut out the booklet cover and cut apart the text strips. Glue the booklet cover onto a sheet of construction paper. Glue each text strip to the bottom of a sheet of paper; then duplicate the pages. Staple the pages together behind the booklet cover; then have the child illustrate each page. Next, set shallow pans of paint at a center along with a supply of lemons that have been cut in half—some horizontally, some vertically. Invite the child to decorate the cover of his booklet with lemon prints. When the paint is dry, encourage him to share his artwork and practice reading his book to his classmates.

Hint: *For best results, let the cut lemons air-dry for about an hour before printing.*

Lemon, Lemonade!
by ___Oliver___

First you take the lemons and you cut 'em.
You cut 'em.

Lemons and Limes Everywhere!

Lemon-fresh bleach. Lime-flavored tortilla chips. Lemon-scented furniture polish. So many products have added a lemon or lime twist! Challenge each of your youngsters to find different products at home that have a lemon or lime additive. Have the child illustrate the product, cut out the labels, or bring in advertisements that show the products. Mount each item on a yellow or green cutout; then tape the cutouts to a chart titled " 'Lemon-Aids' and 'Lime-Aids.' " When the chart is complete, step back and count the many ways we use these tangy fruits. Your class might be surprised to find out how much limes and lemons aid us!

"Lemon-Aids" and "Lime-Aids"

SODA · cake · cookies · PRUNES · gelatin · SHAMPOO

In the Lemon-Limelight

Put your classroom in the limelight with these eye-catching crafts!

You will need:
bright green and yellow construction paper
white or pale yellow construction paper scraps
scissors
glue
yellow and green tissue paper
clear Con-Tact® paper

In advance, cut out a class supply of half circles from yellow and/or bright green construction paper. Then cut out the middle of each half circle (as shown) to create half-circle frames. Fold each middle section in half; then cut through both thicknesses as shown. Next, open the folded piece and cut on the fold line so that you have four wedges in all. Provide each child with a half-circle frame and two wedges. Direct him to glue the wedges to the curved part of the frame. Then have him cut out a construction paper seed and glue it to each wedge. Next, help each child press his frame onto a sheet of clear Con-Tact paper (seed side down). With the sticky side facing up, have the child tear small pieces of yellow or green tissue paper and press them onto the Con-Tact paper. Then help each child cover that side of the project with Con-Tact paper. Trim around the edges. Display the completed projects in a window and let the sun shine in!

Fresh Fruit

It's a well-known fact that lemon juice is often used to prevent fresh fruit from turning brown. Will limes do the same thing? Use this simple science experiment to find out! You will need an apple, lemon juice, and lime juice. Cut three slices from the apple. Thoroughly coat one apple slice with lemon juice; then place it on an index card labeled "Lemon." Coat another slice with lime juice and place it on a card labeled "Lime." Leave the third slice uncoated and place it on a card labeled "Plain." Have students examine the slices and predict what will happen to each one. Record their responses on chart paper labeled "Predictions." After a couple of hours, examine the slices again. (The uncoated piece will turn brown, while the other two will remain relatively unchanged.) Write students' observations on a sheet of chart paper labeled "Observations." Guide students to verbalize conclusions; then write a class conclusion on the chart paper.

Lime   Plain   Lemon

Invisible Ink

Here's a clever home-school connection that may thrill parents as much as children. Begin with a class demonstration of this mysterious activity. Using lemon juice, paint a picture or a message on a sheet of white construction paper. When the juice is dry and no longer visible, place the paper under several sheets of newspaper. Heat an iron to high (no steam); then iron over the newspaper. After several minutes the lemon juice will turn brown and the painting will begin to appear. Show your youngsters the final result and encourage them to guess why that happened. (See the explanation below.)

After the class demonstration, provide each child with a sheet of white construction paper and a copy of the parent note on page 53. Direct him to glue the note to the back of his paper. Then have him use lemon juice to paint a picture on the front. When the lemon juice is dry, have the child take his paper home for an adult to iron. What a juicy idea!

Here's why: *The part of the paper that absorbed the lemon juice burns at a lower temperature than the plain paper does.*

First you take the lemons and you cut 'em.
You cut 'em.

Then you take the lemons and you squeeze 'em.
You squeeze 'em.

Then you add the sugar and the water,
The water.

Then you drop in ice cubes and you stir it.
You stir it.

Pour yourself a glass and you drink it.
You drink it.

Lemon, lemonade—yeah!
Lemon, lemonade—yeah!

Lemon, Lemonade!

by _____

Dear Parents,
   We are learning all about lemons and limes and the many ways we use them. Your child has painted the other side of this paper with invisible ink made from lemon juice. To reveal your child's work, place the paper under several layers of newspaper. With an iron set on high (no steam), iron over the newspaper until the ink begins to appear. How did this happen? Your child can tell you! Have fun!

                              Sincerely,

Marvelous Moon

Launch your youngsters into a totally new atmosphere of learning! Lift off for the moon in 10, 9, 8...

ideas by Bambina L. Merriman

Moonlight!

How does anybody—real or pretend—act in the light of the moon? Dav Pilkey offers one enchanting perspective in *The Moonglow Roll-O-Rama* (Orchard Books). After sharing this book with your students, shine a little moonlight into your own classroom! Tape a large white paper moon on a wall. Turn off all the lights; then have one child shine a flashlight on the moon cutout as the whole class sings and acts out the song below. Each time you repeat the song, ask children to replace the underlined word with a new action word, such as *jump, float, climb, dance,* or *roll.* Then invite students to sing and act out each new verse. (Also choose a new flashlight volunteer as desired.)

(sung to the tune of "Skip to My Lou")

[Skate], [skate], [skate] to the moon,
[Skate], [skate], [skate] to the moon,
[Skate], [skate], [skate] to the moon,
[Skate] to the moon tonight.

Home, Home on the Moon

What would it be like to live on the moon? Youngsters will stretch their imaginations as they author this class book that responds to that very question! In advance, cut out a class supply of circular booklet pages. Also cut out two white or gray construction paper covers. Title and color the front cover similar to the one shown. Introduce this activity by sharing Martha Alexander's charming *You're a Genius, Blackboard Bear* (Candlewick Press). After discussing the story—and where it leaves off!—give each child a booklet page and ask her to write about and illustrate what she thinks it might be like to live on the moon. Stack the completed pages between the covers; then staple along the left side. During a group time, encourage each child to share her page.

The Man in the Moon

Who is that man in the moon anyway? When looking at a big, bright full moon, many people think they see the face of a man—or sometimes other things, such as a rabbit or a bird! Long ago people actually believed there was a man living in the moon. Today we know that the variations in the moon's surface are what cause the "pictures" that appear there. Get your youngsters into creating their own original moon designs by mixing up a batch of the Space Gak below. Put the gak in a sensory tub; then invite children to stop by and create an original moon design. Encourage each child to ask a couple of classmates to take a look at his creation to see what they see in his moon.

Space Gak

Materials:
1 c. white glue
1 c. liquid starch
several drops of food coloring

Directions:
Mix the glue and starch in a bowl. Add several drops of food coloring. Stir until the mixture becomes firm.

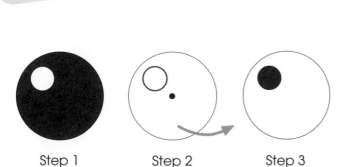

Step 1   Step 2   Step 3

Hello, Moon! Good-Bye, Moon!

It won't be just a phase of learning as your youngsters use their moon-phase wheels to show the different phases of the moon! In advance, make tracers by duplicating page 57 several times onto poster board. Then cut out the patterns. To introduce this activity, share a book about the moon's phases, such as *Armadillo Ray* or *The Squirrel and the Moon* (see the booklist on page 56). Extend the story by following the directions below to help each child make his own moon-phase wheel.

1. Trace the large circle onto black construction paper. Cut along all traced lines, including the inner circle.
2. Trace the large circle (including the inner circle) onto white construction paper. Cut along the outer circle; do *not* cut out the smaller circle.
3. Trace the small circle once onto black construction paper. Cut out the pattern. Then glue the small black circle on the traced area of the large white circle.
4. Position the large black circle on top of the white one and secure them together in the middle with a brad.
5. Draw stars (and/or apply star stickers) on the black wheel to resemble the night sky.

Moon Sculptures

These glow-in-the-dark moon sculptures will get your little ones involved in some hands-on galactic fun! In advance, purchase (or have parents donate) Crayola® Model Magic® nontoxic, air-drying modeling compound. Show your students some moon pictures from a nonfiction book such as *The Moon* by Lesley Sims (Raintree Steck-Vaughn Publishers). Give each child a fist-sized amount of modeling compound and have him roll it into a ball. Then have him use his fingers or an unsharpened pencil to make the surface bumpy and full of mountains, craters, and valleys like the real moon. Allow the sculptures to dry overnight. Then have each student paint his moon with nontoxic glow-in-the-dark paint. Encourage each child to take his moon home to keep in his room at night.

Moon Munchies

These moon munchies are as lumpy and bumpy as the surface of the moon—but probably a bit more tasty! Enlist the help of your little moon explorers to whip up a batch of these delicious moon munchies.

Give each child a baking cup and ask him to write his name on the outside. Melt the white chocolate in a large microwave-safe bowl. Stir in the remaining ingredients until everything is well coated. Then have each child scoop a large spoonful of the mixture into his baking cup. Chill until the mixture sets (about half an hour). Makes approximately 25 servings.

Ingredients for one batch:
24 oz. white baking chocolate
1 c. peanuts
1 c. mini pretzels
10-oz. bag M&M's® candies
10-oz. bag mini marshmallows
paper baking cups
serving spoon

Moon Books!

And If the Moon Could Talk
By Kate Banks
Published by Frances Foster Books

Armadillo Ray
By John Beifuss
Published by Chronicle Books

By the Light of the Moon
By Kelli C. Foster & Gina C. Erickson
Published by Barron's Educational Series, Inc.

Cabbage Moon
By Tim Chadwick
Published by Orchard Books

I'll Catch the Moon
By Nina Crews
Published by Greenwillow Books

The Moon Book
By Gail Gibbons
Published by Holiday House, Inc.

Moondance
By Frank Asch
Published by Scholastic Inc.

No Moon, No Milk!
By Chris Babcock
Published by Crown Publishers, Inc.

The Squirrel and the Moon
By Eleonore Schmid
Published by North-South Books Inc.

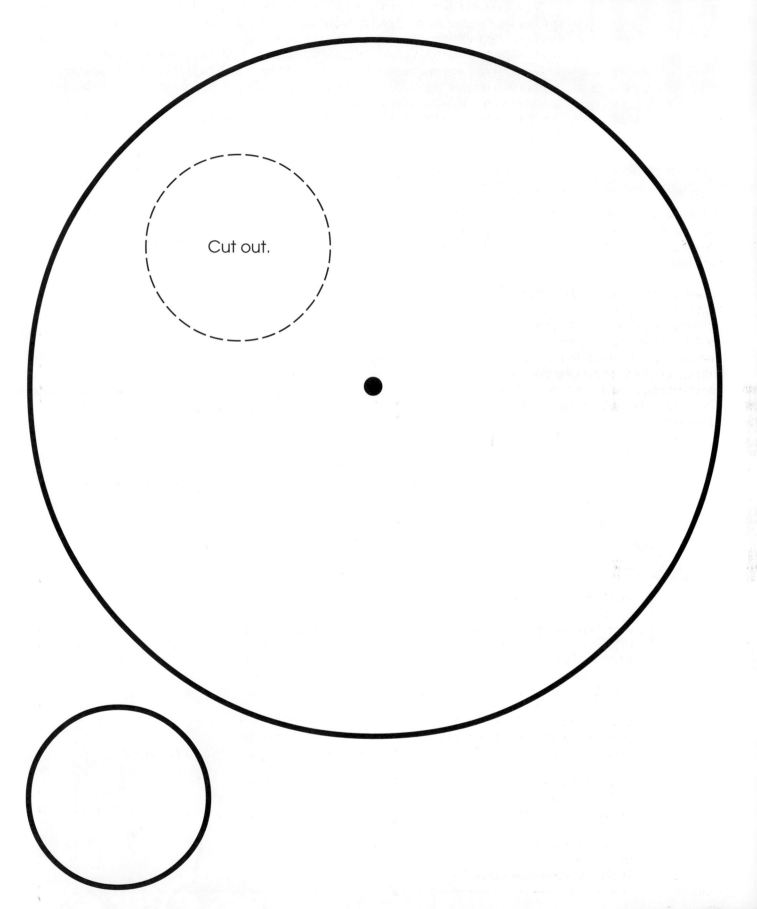

Cut out.

Oodles of Noodles

Learning "pasta-bilities" are bubbling over with these curriculum-related noodle activities.

ideas by Vicki Dabrowka

bow tie	spiral	shell
elbow	wheel	spaghetti
tube	lasagna	oh

Noodles by Name

Take a stroll down the pasta aisle of your local grocery store to discover the vast variety of noodles! Then purchase a wide assortment of them. To prepare for this activity, create a noodle chart. Use craft glue to glue each noodle type to a sheet of poster board. Label each noodle with its name or a description of its shape. (For example, you might use "bow tie" instead of "farfalle.") Display the chart. As you say the name of a noodle, ask children to use their knowledge of noodles and letter sounds to find the noodle on the chart. After each noodle has been introduced, have students read aloud the noodle names together. Save the chart and your noodle collection for other activities in this unit.

I Like Noodles!

Which noodles are the favorites? Find out with this laughable language experience. To prepare, copy the rhyme (right) onto chart paper. Then label a separate notecard with the plural of each noodle on the chart (from "Noodles by Name"). Display the word cards along with the chart and rhyme. After introducing the rhyme, invite one child at a time to find the word card for his favorite noodle. Then have the class repeat the rhyme, replacing *noodles* with the child's noodle choice as he holds his card over the printed word each time it appears. This activity is sure to leave youngsters with a tongue-twisted craving for their noodle favorites!

I Like Noodles
Noodles for breakfast.
Noodles for lunch.
Noodles for dinner.
And even for brunch!

Noodles to squish.
Noodles to crunch.
My, oh my,
I like noodles a bunch!

Pass the Noodles, Please

Serve up a healthy portion of sorting and counting skills with this simple center activity. First, gather your noodle assortment and chart (from "Noodles by Name"). Sort out the noodle types that can be served with a small scoop. Put the "scoopable" noodles in a large pot; then place the pot in a center along with a few small bowls. To do this activity, a child scoops out some noodles into her bowl. She then sorts the noodles and makes a real-object graph with them. Of which noodle type is there the most? What's the name of that noodle? (Refer to the chart.) How many of that type of noodle do you have? What are the names of the other noodles in your graph?

Noodle Song

Here's a little noodle tune that is overflowing with creative-writing opportunities. Sing the song to the right together. Once your children get the hang of it, ask them to think of all kinds of crazy noodle combinations. Then give each child a turn to substitute his own noodle idea for the fourth line of the verse.

Suggested substitutes for line four of the verse: *"Served with eggs and raisin bran," "Served with toast and homemade jam,"* and *"Served with peas and chicken soup."*

Noodle Song

(sung to the tune of "Yankee Doodle")

Verse:
I love noodles,
Yes, I do!
Noodles every day.
[Served with milk or chocolate sauce],
Or any other way!

Chorus:
Noodle doodle, yes, I am!
Anyway I can.
I love noodles every day,
For I'm a noodle fan!

Served with toast and homemade jam.

Noodle Centers

Enhance your centers with these neat noodle activities to reinforce a variety of concepts and skills.

Noodle Art

Who needs a paintbrush when a noodle will do? In advance, cook a supply of spaghetti noodles according to the package directions, adding a few drops of cooking oil to prevent sticking. Drain the noodles; then rinse them in cold water. Place the cold noodles in your art center along with a supply of art paper and several trays of paint. Have a child dip a noodle in paint and then swirl it around on her paper to create a design. Encourage her to use a different noodle for each different paint color. If desired, have her sprinkle glitter on her painting while it is still wet. When the paint is dry, mount each picture on a colorful sheet of construction paper and display it in your class art gallery.

Wiggle Words

Wiggle some letter and word recognition skills out of your children with this fun fine-motor activity. To prepare, cook a supply of spaghetti noodles according to the package directions; then drain and rinse the noodles with cold water. (Or use the leftover noodles from "Noodle Art.") Put the noodles in your writing center along with large laminated word and letter cards. Then invite each child to visit the center to make noodle tracings of the letters or words. Or have older pairs of students work this way: One child picks a card and names the letter or spells the word on it. Then his partner arranges the noodles on a laminated sheet of construction paper to form the letter or word. Finally, the pair compares the noodle model to the card and makes any necessary corrections. Encourage partners to switch roles for each round of play.

Please Don't Move the Noodles!

Steady hands are required for this challenging small-group game of fine-motor skill! (It's adapted from the traditional game of Pick Up Sticks.) To prepare, gather a handful of long, dry noodles, such as spaghetti. Grasp the noodles in a fist and place one end of the noodle bunch on the table. Then gently open your grasp and let the noodles drop to the table (or floor). The first player attempts to pick up a noodle without moving any other noodles. If she succeeds, she keeps that noodle and continues playing until she moves an untouched one. If she does not succeed, play continues in the same manner with the next player. Keep playing until all the noodles have been picked up. If desired, have each child count her noodles to determine the score.

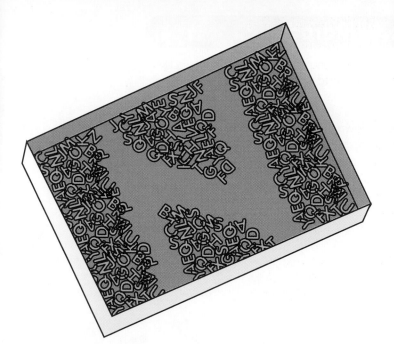

Noodle Doodles

ABCs and 123s are right at your children's fingertips with this idea! To begin, cover the bottom of a shirt box with dry letter noodles; then place the box in your writing center along with a display of letters and numerals. Invite each child to visit the center to practice finger-writing his letters and numerals in the noodles. For an additional sensory experience, put a large flat pan of drained, cooked letter noodles in the center. Then have each student dip his finger in water and "write" in the noodles. (Periodically mist the noodles with water to keep them from sticking together.) Cool noodle doodles!

Noodle Noises

Here's a shake-and-match game that's perfect for fine-tuning listening skills. To prepare, gather ten lidded yogurt containers and your noodle assortment (from "Noodles by Name" on page 58). Then select up to five different noodle types. Make shaker sets by putting each noodle type into two different containers, filling each one equally. For self-checking purposes, attach matching stickers to the bottom of each shaker in a set. Then place the lidded shakers in your listening center. To use, have each child try to match the shakers by sound only. Then ask him to check his work by looking at the stickers. Finally, invite him to open each container to discover which noodle type creates each sound.

Noodle Match

Get all those little fingers warmed up for this sensory activity. Put a cup or two of your dry noodle assortment in a drawstring bag. Place the bag in a center. To do this activity, have a child put his hand in the bag—no peeking! Ask him to feel around in the noodle assortment until he thinks he has two or more matching noodles in his hand. Then have him pull them out to see. Have him continue in the same manner until he has five sets of matching noodles.

Patterns on Parade

These noodle patterns can be as simple or as complex as each child would like! Provide a variety of dry noodles, sentence strips, and craft glue in a center. Invite each child to create a noodle pattern on a sentence strip. During a group time, encourage each child to share his pattern with the group. When each child shares his pattern, ask the class to name the pattern shown (AB, AAB, etc.). Then invite children to create a movement pattern to go with that pattern. For example, they might choose to clap for a bow tie and jump for a wagon wheel. If abilities permit, you could even march around your room according to the movement pattern.

Noodle Counting

Here's a fast-paced counting song to keep your little ones on their counting toes! To prepare, give each singer ten dry noodles. Then have the singers manipulate their noodles to correspond with the song below. Are you ready?

Noodle Counting

(sung to the tune of "Ten Little Indians")

One little, two little, three little noodles.
Four little, five little, six little noodles.
Seven little, eight little, nine little noodles.
Ten little noodles in the pot!

Ten little, nine little, eight little noodles.
Seven little, six little, five little noodles.
Four little, three little, two little noodles.
One little noodle in the pot!

Strega Nona

By Tomie dePaola
Published by Simon and Schuster Books for Young Readers

In this story, an overflowing pasta pot threatens to cover a whole town in noodles! Before sharing this story, stuff a large pot with lengths of white, beige, and/or yellow yarn. Position the lidded pot in front of you as you begin to read the story aloud. When you get to the part where Anthony yells "Stop!" begin tossing out the yarn (noodles) as you continue to read the story. Amidst the giggles and grins, your youngsters are sure to suggest the cure. Once they do, stop tossing the noodles and finish reading the story. Afterward, put the book and the noodle-filled pot in your dramatic-play area. Encourage children to reenact the story when they visit that center.

Noodle-Time Storytime

If your youngsters hunger for more noodle fun, satisfy their cravings with these books about noodles.

Fiction

More Spaghetti, I Say!
By Rita Golden Gelman
Illustrated by Mort Gerberg
Published by Scholastic Inc.

Daddy Makes the Best Spaghetti
By Anna Grossnickle Hines
Published by Clarion Books

Noodles
By Sarah Weeks
Illustrated by David A. Carter
Published by HarperFestival

On Top of Spaghetti
By Tom Glazer
Illustrated by Rob Barber
Published by GoodYearBooks

Nonfiction

From Wheat to Pasta
By Robert Egan
Published by Children's Press

Pasta
By Jillian Powell
Published by Raintree Steck-
   Vaughn Publishers

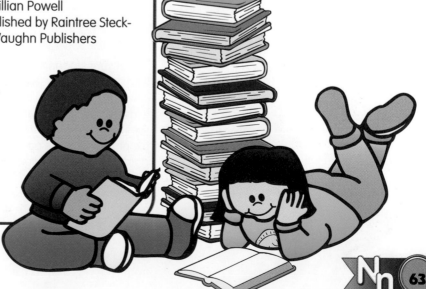

Oh, My— Octopi!

Grab youngsters' attention with this opportunity to explore science, math, literature, and cooking with oodles of octopus fun!

ideas by Chrissy Yuhouse

Octopus Information

Introduce your little ones to octopi with a reading of *Octopus' Den* by Deirdre Langeland (Soundprints). Prior to sharing the book, cut a simple octopus shape from bulletin board paper and post it near your group area. After sharing the book, encourage youngsters to discuss the creature's habitat, defense mechanisms, and changing appearance. Invite them to revisit the illustrations and find the differences in the octopus. What has changed? Its color? Texture? Size? Then ask students to recall some things they have learned about the octopus. Record their observations on your octopus cutout; then keep it on display throughout your unit.

An octopus can change color. —Kami

They squirt ink. —Carlos

They have suckers on their arms. —J.J.

An octopus has eight arms. —Kyra

They live in the ocean. —Callie

Octopus Art

Get your students moving creatively with an art project that will familiarize them with the body parts of an octopus. For each child, fold a 9" x 12" sheet of construction paper in half lengthwise. Draw seven evenly spaced lines on each folded paper as shown. To make an octopus, a child cuts along the predrawn lines to create eight *arms*. (Remind students *not* to cut all the way to the fold of the paper.) Then he paints on *suckers* by holding a small pom-pom with a clothespin and dipping it into paint, then pressing it onto the arms repeatedly. When the paint has dried, roll the paper into a circle with the suckers on the inside and staple the ends together. Next, give each child a construction paper *mantle* (head). Have him draw a face for his octopus and then glue it atop the arms. If desired, curl each arm around a pencil. Then punch two holes at the top of each octopus (on either side of the head). Thread a 20-inch piece of string through the holes and tie it into a loop. Hang these awesome octopi from your classroom ceiling for all to admire!

"Ink-credible"!

No bones about it! Octopi are soft and muscular creatures that lack the protection of teeth, claws, bones, or a shell. What keeps them safe? Your students will be amazed to learn that octopi squirt clouds of ink to protect themselves in times of danger. To prepare for this science activity, gather a glass jar, an eyedropper, a small plastic octopus, and a container of thinned black paint. Fill the jar with water and then place the toy octopus inside. Have your little ones estimate the number of "ink" droplets it will take to completely hide the octopus. Then add drops of thinned black paint to the water, counting each drop as you go. When the octopus is hidden, your little scientists will see firsthand an octopus's "ink-credible" defense!

Ollie the Octopus

Keep this fingerplay at arm's length to remind your students about the unique defense mechanism of the octopus.

Ollie the Octopus

Ollie is an octopus who lives beneath the sea.	*Hang hand down.*
Every day he jets from here to there quite happily.	*Move hand back and forth.*
If you spot him anywhere, you'd better stop and think!	*Shake index finger.*
For if he does not know you, he might squirt you with his ink!	*Open hand suddenly.*

In the Dark

Is there an octopus hiding in your classroom? Let your students find out with this gross-motor activity. Use green masking tape to create a large seaweed plant on the floor. Tell your students to be on the lookout for an octopus that might hide in the seaweed. As each student pretends to be a sea creature swimming, squirming, and crawling near the seaweed, turn off the lights and call out, "Octopus ink!" Have your class freeze in place until the cloud of ink disappears. Encourage your little ones to take a quick look around for the mysterious octopus. Hmmm…he must have gotten away! As the mysterious octopus comes and goes, your curious critters will be wiggling and giggling with excitement!

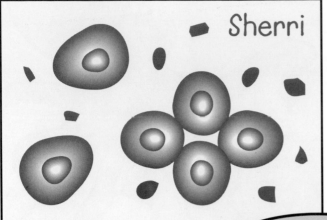
Sherri

Arm Art

This art center idea will have each of your students painting as if she were an octopus! Place white paper, eyedroppers, black tempera paint, and suction cups at a center. Introduce this center by asking your youngsters what body parts an octopus might use to paint a picture. Then encourage each child to paint like an octopus, using the suction cup "suckers" and the black tempera "ink" at the center. After this creative endeavor, your little artists will be stuck on octopi and will want to learn more about their unique features!

Suction Cup Studies

Octopi have hundreds of suckers on their arms. Encourage your little ones to explore suction with this science and math activity. To prepare, create a chart similar to the one shown. Duplicate the chart to make a class supply. You'll also need a class supply of one-inch suction cups. Give each child a copy of the chart and a suction cup, and invite him to test out each surface on the chart for "stickability." Have him draw a picture of an octopus in the yes or no section on the chart or use octopus stickers to indicate his answers. Review students' findings. Then, as a follow-up, have each student take his suction cup and chart home and encourage him to test out other surfaces.

Will it stick? Will it fall? Will the suction cup hold at all?

surface		yes	no
window		🐙	
table		🐙	
carpet			🐙
lunchbox			🐙

Tasty Octopus Arms

Tempt your students' taste buds with these tantalizing octopus arm treats! Purchase refrigerated breadstick dough, a box of Cheerios® cereal, and a jar of blackberry jam. Begin by unrolling the dough and pulling off a strip of dough for each child. Line up the dough strips on a cookie sheet. Next, direct each student to count out ten Cheerios and place them on a dough arm to look like suckers. Bake the treats at 325° for eight to ten minutes. When cool, serve with a little blackberry jam "ink" for a finishing touch. Yum!

Where Is That Octopus?

It's red! It's orange! It's coral! It's a rock! It's an octopus? Remind your youngsters that an octopus can protect itself through camouflage. And not only can it change its color, but it can change its texture as well. Create a display about the amazing, changeable octopus to stimulate your little ones' senses and reinforce this octopus fact.

On a large piece of poster board, use textured materials—such as corduroy, sandpaper, cardboard, foil wrapping paper, and craft foam—to create an ocean scene. Cut rocks, seaweed, coral, and the ocean floor from the various materials. Then cut several simple octopus shapes from the same materials. Encourage youngsters to explore the various colors and textures in the scene. Then ask them to match the octopi to the corresponding surfaces in the scene. Invite them to use Sticky-Tac to place each octopus "in hiding." This exercise is sure to leave youngsters feelin' fine about learning!

Grab an Armful of These Great Books!

An Octopus Is Amazing
By Patricia Lauber
Published by HarperTrophy

Gentle Giant Octopus
By Karen Wallace
Published by Candlewick Press

How to Hide an Octopus & Other Sea Creatures
By Ruth Heller
Published by Price Stern Sloan

Herman the Helper
By Robert Kraus
Published by Aladdin Paperbacks

My Very Own Octopus
By Bernard Most
Published by Harcourt Brace & Company

Follow Me!
By Bethany Roberts
Published by Clarion Books

Oliver's High Five
By Beverly Swerdlow Brown
(Check your school or public library)

Octavia Warms Up
By Barbara Beak
(Check your school or public library)

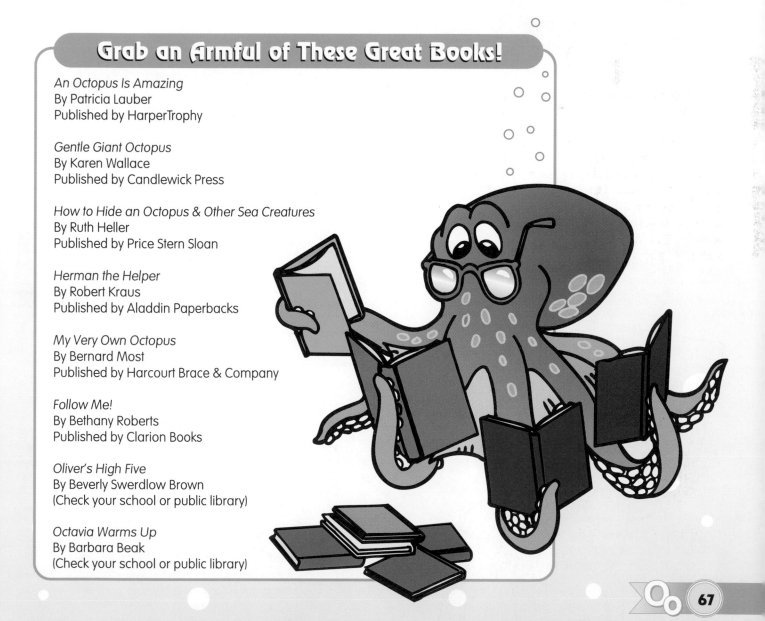

Peeking Into Pockets

Pennies, marbles, and whistles hidden deep in pockets—your little ones bring such tiny treasures to school every day. Stock your own pockets with some teaching treasures when you take a peek at these pocket ideas!

ideas by Vicki Dabrowka

Pocket Pals

Promote your pocket theme by creating a jumbo-sized pocket display with a classroom pocket pal tucked inside. In advance, cut out a large pocket from bulletin board paper and staple the side and bottom edges to a bulletin board. Then place a light-weight stuffed animal into the pocket so it appears to be peeking out of the top. Perpetuate more pocket fun by having a tiny stuffed or bean-filled pal peering out of your own pocket. The next day, ask your school principal to stop by your classroom with the same pal hiding in his or her pocket. Continue this hide-and-seek game with a different school staff person for each of the remaining days of your unit. Youngsters will bounce into school to see who has their pocket pal each day!

Pondering Pockets

So…what's in *your* pocket? Here's a bulletin board that will allow little ones to display their answers to that question! For each child, make a colored construction paper copy of the pocket pattern on page 71. Then ask students to brainstorm things that will fit into a pocket—perhaps by inspecting the contents of their own pockets! Write a response from each child on a separate paper pocket. Give each pocket to its owner and ask the child to write his name, draw (or glue on) a picture to match his idea, and then cut out the pocket shape. Mount these on the bulletin board created for "Pocket Pals" (above).

As a variation for kindergartners, place alphabet cards beside the bulletin board. Invite each child to slip a letter card into the pocket showing an item with the corresponding beginning sound. *M* is for marbles and *K* is for keys—pockets are just full of ABCs!

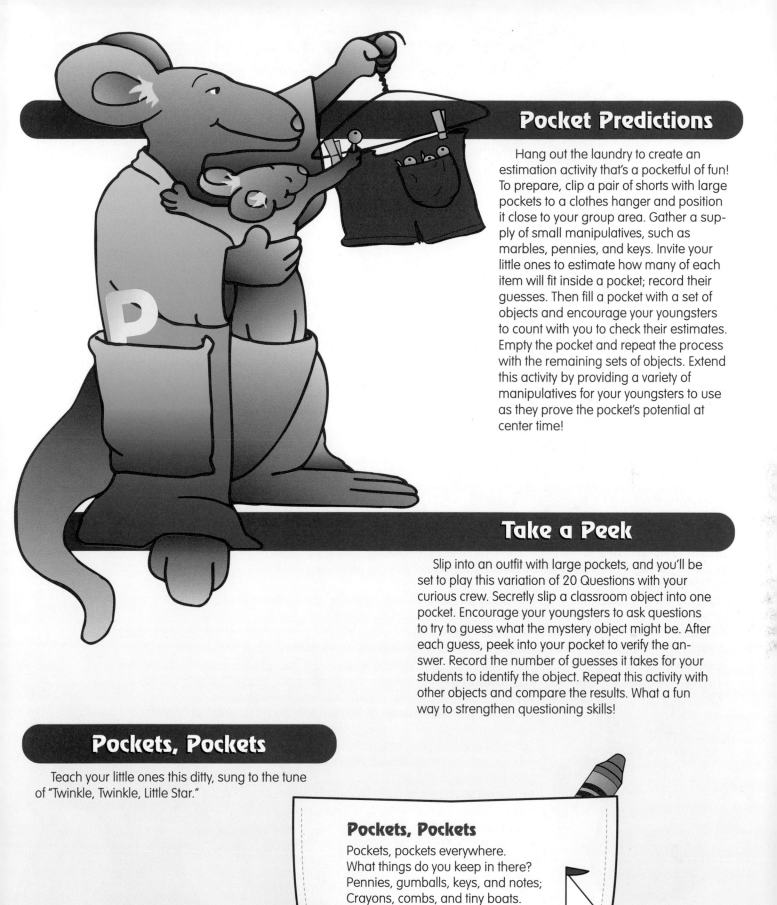

Pocket Predictions

Hang out the laundry to create an estimation activity that's a pocketful of fun! To prepare, clip a pair of shorts with large pockets to a clothes hanger and position it close to your group area. Gather a supply of small manipulatives, such as marbles, pennies, and keys. Invite your little ones to estimate how many of each item will fit inside a pocket; record their guesses. Then fill a pocket with a set of objects and encourage your youngsters to count with you to check their estimates. Empty the pocket and repeat the process with the remaining sets of objects. Extend this activity by providing a variety of manipulatives for your youngsters to use as they prove the pocket's potential at center time!

Take a Peek

Slip into an outfit with large pockets, and you'll be set to play this variation of 20 Questions with your curious crew. Secretly slip a classroom object into one pocket. Encourage your youngsters to ask questions to try to guess what the mystery object might be. After each guess, peek into your pocket to verify the answer. Record the number of guesses it takes for your students to identify the object. Repeat this activity with other objects and compare the results. What a fun way to strengthen questioning skills!

Pockets, Pockets

Teach your little ones this ditty, sung to the tune of "Twinkle, Twinkle, Little Star."

Pockets, Pockets

Pockets, pockets everywhere.
What things do you keep in there?
Pennies, gumballs, keys, and notes;
Crayons, combs, and tiny boats.
Pockets, pockets everywhere—
Aren't you glad you have a pair?

Pocketed Puppet

Your little ones will enjoy making their own pocketed pals as they discover there are animals that have built-in pockets! Explain to your students that kangaroos, koalas, and opossums belong to a family of animals known as *marsupials*. Mother marsupials are special because they have a pocketlike pouch in which to carry their young. If desired, share photos of kangaroos or other marsupials from an encyclopedia or nonfiction book. Then create a mama kangaroo puppet starring each child's finger as a joey in the pouch!

To prepare, duplicate the kangaroo and pouch patterns on page 71 onto construction paper to make a class supply. Have each child glue her kangaroo onto poster board for durability before cutting it out. Cut out the opening on each child's puppet. Then have each child decorate her kangaroo with markers. Help her position the pouch over the opening and tape it in place, as shown. Use a marker to dot each child's index finger with facial features; then have her slide her finger into the hole on the kangaroo puppet. Hippity-hop!

Operation Overalls

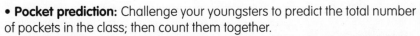

An overall good time will be had when you plan an Overalls Day to close your pocket unit! Send home a note requesting that each child wear overalls (or clothing with several pockets) to school. Then let the pocket play get under way!

- **Pocket prediction:** Challenge your youngsters to predict the total number of pockets in the class; then count them together.
- **Pocket graph:** Make a graph showing the number of pockets each child has on his clothing. In advance, make a class supply of the pocket shape on page 71 to use as graph markers. Ask each child to write his name on a cutout and tape it on the correct column on the graph. Then discuss the results, emphasizing the concepts of *more, fewer,* and *equal.*
- **Pocket problem solving:** Make up addition and subtraction stories involving your students' pockets. For example: "How many pockets do Sam and Tina have all together?" or "Susie has six pockets and three are full. How many empty pockets does she have?"
- **Pocket snack:** What is the perfect pocket treat? A pita, of course! In advance, purchase a class supply of small pita bread and cheese slices. Cut each pita in half to create a pocket; then fill with cheese. If desired, microwave these snacks for ten seconds to melt the cheese. Invite youngsters to enjoy their snacks while you read aloud *A Pocket for Corduroy* by Don Freeman (Viking Press).

Pocket Pattern

Use with "Pondering Pockets" on page 68 and "Operation Overalls" on page 70.

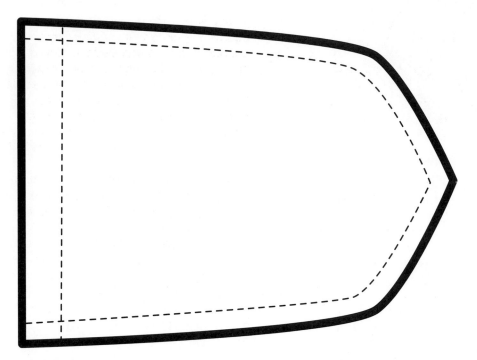

Kangaroo and Pouch Patterns

Use with "Pocketed Puppet" on page 70.

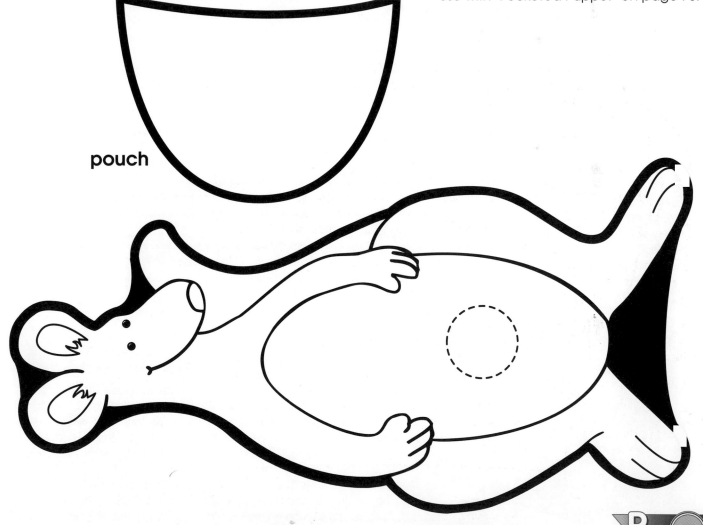

pouch

Cozy Quilts

"Needle" little creative material to teach your youngsters about quilts? Use these crafty ideas that cover a variety of subject areas!

ideas by Vicki Dabrowka

A Comforting Beginning

Create a warm, colorful classroom environment by adding special touches to your bulletin boards, doors, dramatic-play areas, and more! Before starting your unit, purchase (or borrow) fabric, quilted fabric pieces, and finished quilts. Use the suggestions below to blanket your classroom in comfort and warmth!

- Use strips of fabric to make colorful borders for your bulletin boards and/or doors.
- Liven up your dramatic-play area by making placemats and tablecloths with pieces of cloth taped around the edges to prevent fraying.
- Drape a large quilt (or fabric piece) over three sides of a table, creating a cozy tent area where your little ones can read or nap.
- Make quilt-themed nametags by cutting out squares or rectangles from fabric. Use a permanent marker to print each student's name on a separate nametag. Then cover the cloth on both sides with a clear adhesive covering. To wear, attach these nametags with safety pins.
- Staple fabric squares to a bulletin board to make a quilt background.

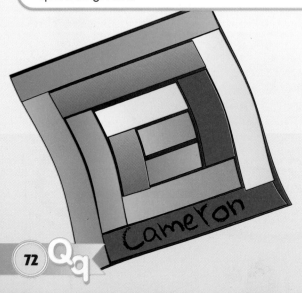

Log Cabin Quilt Squares

Thread some Amish culture into your quilt studies with this center activity. In advance, cut a class supply of ten-inch squares from black construction paper. Also cut different-colored one-inch-wide construction paper strips. Then place them at a center along with the black squares, scissors, and glue. To introduce this activity, read *Reuben and the Quilt* by Merle Good (Good Books) and discuss how the long strips of fabric were used in the story. Then, when a child visits this center, have him glue the paper strips onto a black square. Encourage him to cut the strips so that they do not overlap on his square. When the glue is dry, label the quilt. These stunning designs make a brilliant classroom display!

squeeeeeeeeeeeeeeeeeeeeek

Amish Quilt Squares

Review *Reuben and the Quilt* by Merle Good (Good Books) and then facilitate a discussion on the colors that the Amish people chose for their clothes. Tell students that they are going to help each other make a quilt in the same way the Amish work together to accomplish their tasks. In advance, make several stencils by folding six-inch tagboard circles in fourths and then cutting out a shape (similar to the one shown) from each circle. Place the opened stencils in a center along with large pom-poms or sponge squares, a shallow dish of dark purple paint, and a supply of blue and green four-inch construction paper squares. Have each child press the stencil on top of his square while he uses a pom-pom or sponge to dab paint inside the shape. When the paint is dry, punch holes in the squares as shown and tie them together using lengths of dark-colored yarn. Then attach all the quilt pieces to a bulletin board covered with black construction paper. What a charming Amish quilt!

Miniature Hawaiian Quilts

Did you know that traditional Hawaiian quilts only have two colors in them? *Luka's Quilt* by Georgia Guback (Greenwillow Books) illustrates this fact in an endearing story. After sharing the book, discuss how Hawaiian quilts are different from others your youngsters have learned about *(they use only two colors)*. At a center, instruct each child to fold a sheet of construction paper in half lengthwise. Then have him cut out designs from the open side of the folded paper. Next, have him cut out designs from the folded side. Then have each child carefully unfold his paper and then glue it onto a different color of construction paper. That's traditional Hawaiian style!

Friendship Quilt Squares

These personalized quilt squares will bring a sense of ownership and camaraderie to your classroom! Begin by telling children that long ago, when a group of people made a *friendship quilt* for a gift, each person would write or stitch her name on the square that she was contributing to the quilt. At a center, have each student print his name on a large white construction paper square. Then have him use pastel-colored tempera paint and sponge shapes to make a pattern of prints around his name. When the paint is dry, hang these personalized quilt squares on your door for a fascinating friendship display!

Treasures of the Heart

Quilts—like stories—become more meaningful when passed from one generation to the next. Travel through the years and across the miles with a very special quilt in *The Quilt Story* by Tony Johnston (G. P. Putnam's Sons). After reading and discussing the story, ask students if they have things at home that are very special to them. Then invite them (with parental permission) to bring their treasured items to school. Make a classroom museum by covering a table with fabric. Encourage youngsters to make name cards for their items and then display their family heirlooms for all to see. Are there any quilts or blankets in the bunch?

Sara

Keepsake Quilt Booklet

After studying various types of quilts, it's time to go back to the basics with these cute booklets! In advance, make a class supply of the booklet patterns on page 75. Cut a class supply of 4" x 5" construction paper covers. Also cut fabric scraps into one-inch squares. Use the directions below to help your students complete their booklet pages. Send the finished booklets home with your students and encourage them to snuggle up with their families, read their booklets, and teach family members a stitch or two about different types of quilts!

Cover: Print your name on the cover. Glue on patches of fabric to decorate the cover.

Page 1: Glue on four one-inch squares to create a bigger square.

Page 2: Glue colored thread onto the page.

Page 3: Glue a stretched-out cotton ball or Poly-Fil® filling to the page.

Page 4: Decorate this page by gluing on heart-shaped buttons, stickers, or sequins.

Binding the booklet: Stack the pages in order between the covers and staple.

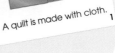

A quilt is made with cloth. 1

A quilt is made with thread. 2

A quilt is made with filling. 3

A quilt is made with love. 4

Use with "Keepsake Quilt Booklet" on page 74.

A quilt is made with cloth. 1	A quilt is made with thread. 2
A quilt is made with filling. 3	A quilt is made with love. 4

Ready for Raccoons!

Black masks and ringed tails are just two of the telltale features of these cute and curious critters. Use the ideas in this unit to learn more!

ideas by Suzanne Moore

Raccoon Report

Spark students' curiosity about raccoons with these fascinating facts.

- A raccoon has a patch of black fur on its face that looks like a mask.
- A raccoon's tail has black rings around it and a black tip.
- A raccoon usually lives in the woods near water but can be found in other places too.
- A raccoon eats lots of different foods, such as fish, frogs, turtles, bird eggs, insects, nuts, corn, and discarded food in garbage cans.
- A raccoon has very nimble fingers. It can even turn handles and open doors!
- A raccoon likes to handle its food and other objects, especially in the water.
- A raccoon can make a variety of sounds to communicate its feelings.
- A raccoon is *nocturnal*, meaning it is most active at night.

Feels Just Fine

Raccoons are known for the fact that they like to play with their food and small objects, usually rubbing them between their palms. Since their fingers become even more sensitive when wet, they especially enjoy playing with their food in water. To provide youngsters with a similar sensory experience, convert your water table into a raccoon's water paradise. To begin, put a layer of sand in your water table and add water. Scatter some pebbles and shells in the water; then add a collection of small rubber and plastic animals to represent those found in a raccoon's diet (see "Raccoon Report"). When children visit this center, encourage them to pretend to be raccoons, exploring the feel of things in the water. If desired, place corncobs, nuts, plastic eggs, and fruit near the table to represent other raccoon foods. Then invite the child to immerse the items in the water, raccoon-style, for more sensory fun. Go ahead and get your fingers wet—it feels just fine!

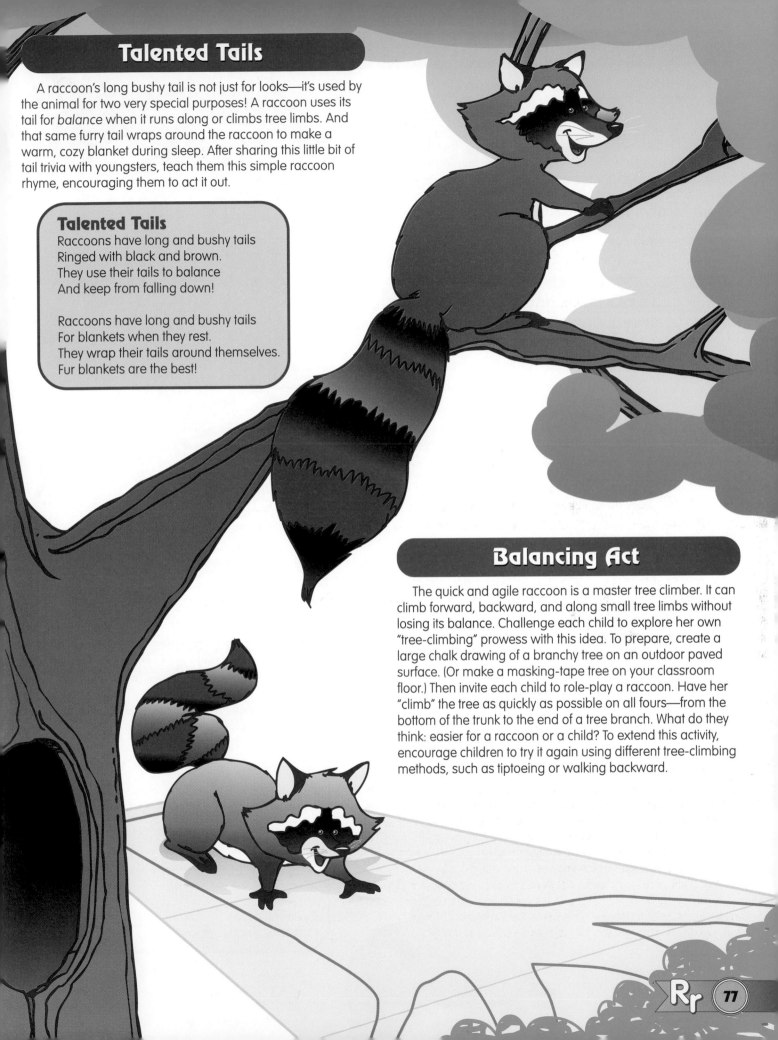

Talented Tails

A raccoon's long bushy tail is not just for looks—it's used by the animal for two very special purposes! A raccoon uses its tail for *balance* when it runs along or climbs tree limbs. And that same furry tail wraps around the raccoon to make a warm, cozy blanket during sleep. After sharing this little bit of tail trivia with youngsters, teach them this simple raccoon rhyme, encouraging them to act it out.

Talented Tails

Raccoons have long and bushy tails
Ringed with black and brown.
They use their tails to balance
And keep from falling down!

Raccoons have long and bushy tails
For blankets when they rest.
They wrap their tails around themselves.
Fur blankets are the best!

Balancing Act

The quick and agile raccoon is a master tree climber. It can climb forward, backward, and along small tree limbs without losing its balance. Challenge each child to explore her own "tree-climbing" prowess with this idea. To prepare, create a large chalk drawing of a branchy tree on an outdoor paved surface. (Or make a masking-tape tree on your classroom floor.) Then invite each child to role-play a raccoon. Have her "climb" the tree as quickly as possible on all fours—from the bottom of the trunk to the end of a tree branch. What do they think: easier for a raccoon or a child? To extend this activity, encourage children to try it again using different tree-climbing methods, such as tiptoeing or walking backward.

Paper Bag Bandits

Raccoons will scurry around your classroom when little ones create these paper bag puppets. To prepare, gather a class supply of brown paper lunch bags and some white yarn; then duplicate the raccoon patterns on page 79 for each child. To make a puppet, have each child color and cut out the raccoon patterns. Then have her glue each cutout onto her bag (as shown) and then add white yarn whiskers to complete her project. When the glue is dry, invite youngsters to dramatize an imaginary raccoon romp through the city or retell the stories from "Raccoon Readings" with their puppets. Afterward, encourage each child to share her puppet and her raccoon knowledge with her family.

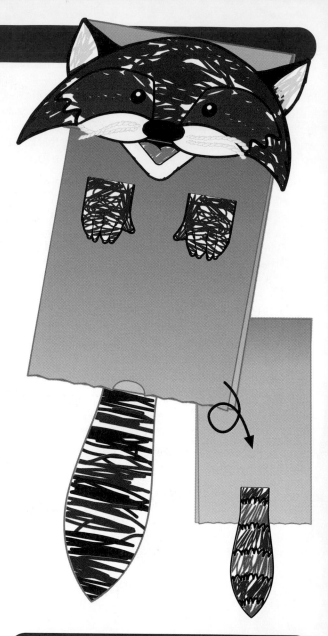

Raccoon Crunchies

Raccoons will eat almost anything, but they *do* have their preferences! Invite your youngsters to help make this crunchy treat (for people) that features some raccoon favorites—peanuts, fruit, and sweets. Yummy!

Raccoon Crunchies

1 c. peanuts
1 c. raisins
1 c. Cheerios® cereal
1 c. M&M's® candy

Mix all the ingredients together in a bowl.
Then crunch and munch away!

Raccoon Readings

Share a couple of clever stories about these cute little critters. Then put the books in your reading center for your curious students to investigate more closely.

The Kissing Hand
By Audrey Penn
Published by Child & Family Press

Timothy Goes to School
By Rosemary Wells
Published by Dial Books for Young Readers

Raccoons and Ripe Corn
By Jim Arnosky
Published by Mulberry Books

face

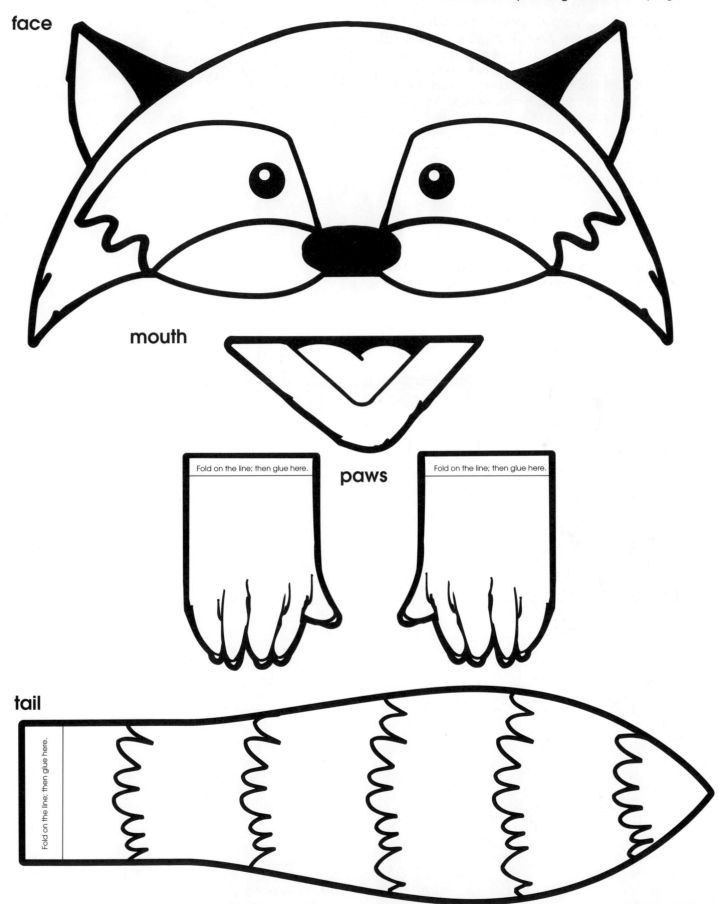

mouth

paws

Fold on the line; then glue here.

Fold on the line; then glue here.

tail

Fold on the line; then glue here.

A Super Sandwich Selection

Satisfy your youngsters' appetites for learning with these scrumptious sandwich ideas!

ideas by Rosemary Kesse

So, What *Is* a Sandwich?

Fill your little ones' plates with heaps of sandwich knowledge! Begin by having students name words or phrases that describe a sandwich. Record the responses on a sheet of chart paper. Then explain to students that the word *sandwich* means "to insert or put between." Use classroom items to demonstrate the concept of sandwiching. Then ask your students to name some fillings and types of bread that might be used for sandwiches. Add these ideas to your chart paper. Encourage students to think of as many types of sandwich foods as they can (hot dog, hoagie, hamburger, pita, gyro, ice-cream sandwich, etc.). Your youngsters' tummies will be growling after this brainstorming session!

Sandwiches

– big	**Fillings**
– brown	peanut butter
– have bread	tuna salad
– can have pickles	jelly
– square	cheese
– yummy!	ham
– have cheese in them	
	Bread
<u>Kinds of Sandwiches</u>	white
hamburgers	wheat
PB & J	sub roll
ice-cream sandwich	pita
cookie sandwich	
hot dog	

Setting Up a Sandwich Shop

Open the doors to learning by inviting your little ones to help you transform your dramatic-play area into a sandwich shop! Enlist the help of parents to supply your classroom sandwich shop with desired items (see the following list for suggestions). When all the items are gathered, encourage your youngsters to arrange the area. Then see "Open for Business!" on page 81 for some ways to make this sandwich shop a stunning success!

Plastic plates, dishes, trays, and cups
Pretend bread made from $1/2$"-thick foam
Pretend meat, cheese, lettuce, and pickles made from thin craft foam or felt
Clean plastic mustard, ketchup, and mayonnaise bottles
A calculator or toy cash register and play money
Notepads and markers for taking orders
Tablecloths (cut to fit the size of small tables) and cloth napkins
Plastic vases with artificial flowers for each table
Cloth aprons
A small dustpan and broom
Clean rags or sponges
Sterilized Styrofoam® trays
White paper lunch bags

Open for Business!

In order to have a successful sandwich-making business, your youngsters will have to serve up generous helpings of imagination. Use the following suggestions to help get your shop up and running!

- Invite students to offer name suggestions for the shop. Print each name idea on a sheet of chart paper. Then have students vote on their favorite.
- Duplicate the sign pattern on page 83. Have your students make Daily Special signs. Also encourage them to work cooperatively to create a poster board storefront sign.
- Have little ones make their own menus using construction paper, markers, and food pictures from magazines. If desired, provide sample menus from local restaurants to tempt youngsters' imaginations.
- Have youngsters use poster board strips and construction paper to design their own headband hats to be used when they are busy in the kitchen.
- What would a restaurant be without take-out and delivery bags? Have each student print the name of the shop on a white lunch bag. Then have him use markers and various art supplies to decorate the bag.
- After a busy day in a sandwich shop, there's lots to clean up! Have students use sponges to wipe down tables and counters. A few sweeps of a broom will put the finishing touch on a fabulous day of work!

Ketchup, Please!

Some sandwiches just aren't complete without a squirt and a squeeze of ketchup or mustard. Your students won't be able to bottle their enthusiasm as they create unique art projects with counterfeit condiments! In advance, make two enlarged construction paper copies of the bread pattern on page 83 for each student. Then fill a clean plastic ketchup bottle with red tempera paint and a clean plastic mustard bottle with yellow tempera paint. Have each student squirt lines and dots of paint onto one paper bread slice. Then have him place the other bread slice on top and press the sandwich slices together. Assist the child in separating the slices to reveal a colorful surprise. Show off these sandwich slices for a delectable display!

An Alphabet Sandwich

Tempt your little chefs' creativity and language skills with this one-of-a-kind class book! To prepare the front and back covers, make two construction paper copies of the bread pattern on page 83. Label one slice as shown; then laminate the covers. Make poster board templates of circles, squares, and triangles. Finally, label a sheet of chart paper with all the letters of the alphabet.

At a group time, explain to your little ones that you're going to build an alphabet sandwich. Ask the first child to name a sandwich ingredient—serious or silly—that begins with the letter A. Print her response on your chart paper. Then have the next child name an ingredient that begins with B. Keep going until you have a complete list. Then ask each student to choose a shape template, trace it onto white construction paper, cut it out, and illustrate her named ingredient on the resulting page. Stack all the pages in alphabetical order between the laminated covers. Punch holes along the left side of each page and cover; then bind the book with lengths of yarn. This interesting creation is one your youngsters will "chews" to read again and again!

Savory Smells

What's in a sandwich? In this activity, the nose knows! In advance, prepare several plastic containers, each containing a different aromatic sandwich item—such as ketchup, ham, bologna, mustard, a dill pickle, jelly, peanut butter, and a green pepper. Gather your group and teach them the song below. Bring out the containers and inform your youngsters that each one contains a sandwich ingredient that they must identify. The only trick is they have to use *only* their noses! Sing the song, open the container, and have students close their eyes and try to identify the ingredient by smelling it. After each child has had a turn, reveal the ingredient. Sing the song again, using the next ingredient. Then spread the news—your students are super sandwich sleuths!

The Sandwich Song
(sung to the tune of "I'm a Little Teapot")

I'm a little sandwich on your plate.
I have something special, just you wait.
Is it bologna? Is it ham?
Can you guess just what I am?

Sandwich Snacktime

When your little ones have the munchies, let them chomp on these simple shape sandwiches! Follow the directions below to create a variety of snacks to enjoy on different days of your sandwich unit.

Circle Sandwiches: Cut bologna and cheese with a circle cookie cutter and stack them between round crackers.
Square Sandwiches: Serve pairs of saltine crackers with cream cheese filling.
Triangle Sandwiches: Cut simple cheese sandwiches on the diagonal to create triangles.
Rectangle Sandwiches: Sandwich peanut butter between rectangular graham cracker sections.

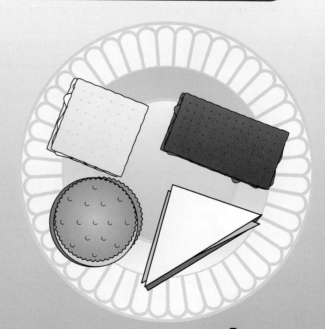

Read 'em and Eat

While youngsters are munching on their shapely sandwiches, share one of these sandwich stories.

Sam's Sandwich
Written by David Pelham
Published by Dutton Books

The Giant Jam Sandwich
Written by John Vernon Lord
Published by Houghton Mifflin Company

Little Bird and the Moon Sandwich
Written by Linda Berkowitz
Published by Crown Publishers, Inc.

Sandwiches!

©2000 The Education Center, Inc. • *Themes From A to Z* • TEC373

Bread Slice Pattern
Use with "An Alphabet Sandwich" and "Ketchup, Please!" on page 81.

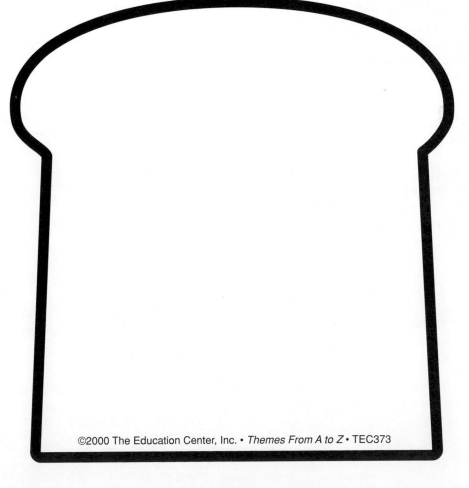

©2000 The Education Center, Inc. • *Themes From A to Z* • TEC373

Teatime!

It's time for a tea party! Invite your little ones to bring their best manners and join you for a cup of teatime fun!

ideas by Elizabeth Fritz

Little Teapot Prop

"I'm a little teapot short and stout…" That's all you'll need to say to inspire a rousing rendition of the traditional song! Gather your youngsters to perform this favorite movement song several times. If desired, delight your class by reading the adventurous version of *I'm a Little Teapot* by Iza Trapani (Charlesbridge Publishing, Inc.). Then invite your youngsters to make a teapot blower for dramatic play. Collect a class supply of party blowers; then duplicate the teapot pattern on page 87 onto heavy paper for each child. Ask each child to color and cut out his teapot. Cut a hole in the spout along the dotted line and insert a blower as shown. Encourage each child to hold his teapot as he recites the song. Then listen to the giggles as your little teapots steam up and blow!

Tea Tray Relay

Steady…set…go! Your little ones will race to perform this balancing act! In advance, collect two plastic trays and two plastic tea sets. To set up the relay lanes, put strips of tape on the floor as shown. Divide your class into two teams and ask each group to stand behind its starting line. Place a tea set on each tray and pass each tray to the first child on each team. Explain the rules of the game (walk, don't run; pick up any dropped item and continue). At your signal, the first child from each team carries her tray to the end of the lane. Then she returns to the starting line and gives her tray to the next player on her team. Continue until all members of both teams have had a turn. Award each participant a ribbon that says "Tea-rific!" What a dashing good time!

Big on Manners

Planning a tea party is a fine opportunity to talk about good manners. Create a class big book to reinforce manners every day! Ask your youngsters to brainstorm a list of different ways to show good manners. Encourage a variety of responses, writing each child's idea on a different sheet of chart paper. Instruct each child to illustrate his example of good manners for his big book page. Then stack all the pages together with a poster board cover titled "We Are BIG on Good Manners!" Staple the book along the left side. Share the story with your students; then place it in your reading center for their further enjoyment—and as a gentle reminder about good manners!

We Are
BIG
on Good Manners!
By Mrs. Daoust's Kindergarten

Alex

Remember to say,
"Thank you."

Teatime Tune

Try this echo song sung to the tune of "Are You Sleeping?" to promote a little good-mannered fun.

Tip your pinky.
Tip your pinky.
Sip your tea.
Sip your tea.
Always use good manners.
Always use good manners.
Just say, "Please."
Just say, "Please."

Tip your pinky.
Tip your pinky.
Hold your cup.
Hold your cup.
Thank you for the tea, ma'am [sir].
Thank you for the tea, ma'am [sir].
Drink it up!
Drink it up!

Designer Tablecloths

Encourage your little ones to create beautiful table covers for their special upcoming tea party. Lay out a large sheet of white bulletin board paper and sets of watercolor paint for each small group of students. If desired, play a recording of soft classical music. Ask your little artists to listen to the music as they paint flowers, rainbows, or nature scenes. Let the table covers dry and lay them aside to add a festive touch to the upcoming tea party.

Sun Tea Science

Treat your youngsters to a teatime science experiment they can drink! In advance, collect a glass gallon jar and six decaffeinated tea bags. Choose a sunny day to gather your little learners for this experiment. To begin, fill the jar with cool water and instruct student helpers to drop the tea bags into it. Cover the container with plastic wrap; then set it in a sunny window. If desired, read *Sun Song* by Jean Marzollo (HarperTrophy). Then explain to the children that the warmth of the sunlight will cause the tea to slowly mix with the water. Check the tea each hour and notice the color. When it reaches a deep golden brown, it's ready to drink. Add ice, sugar, and perhaps a spot of lemon for a cool tea treat! Then have your young scientists repeat the procedure to prepare a pitcher of sun tea to serve at your class tea party.

Easy Tea Cakes

Enlist the help of a parent volunteer to assist your little bakers in making these proper little tea cakes.

Tea Cakes

Ingredients:

2 eggs
1½ c. white sugar
½ c. shortening
4 c. all-purpose flour
1 tsp. baking soda
½ tsp. salt
colored sugar

Preheat oven to 400°. Mix the shortening and sugar together; then add eggs. Mix the dry ingredients together and add to the shortening mixture. Stir until the dough is stiff. Then roll out the dough onto a floured surface and cut out shapes with cookie cutters. Place the shapes on a greased cookie sheet, sprinkle on colored sugar, and bake for eight minutes. Save these tasty treats to serve at your tea party.

A Grand Tea Party

A grand time will be had by all as your youngsters host their very own tea party! In advance, make a simple invitation for each child to take home for a parent, a grandparent, or a special grown-up friend. Ask parent volunteers to supply several ceramic teapots, a variety of tea bags, cups, and napkins. Also ask for help with serving hot tea at the party. (Exercise caution with hot beverages in the classroom and serve children only warm tea.) On the day of the party, invite the children to cover the tables with their painted tablecloths and to set out napkins, the sun tea they prepared, and their homemade tea cakes. Have each child escort his guest to a chair and help serve her refreshments. Finally, ask your students to entertain their guests by performing "I'm a Little Teapot" and "Teatime Tune" (page 85). What a delightful afternoon!

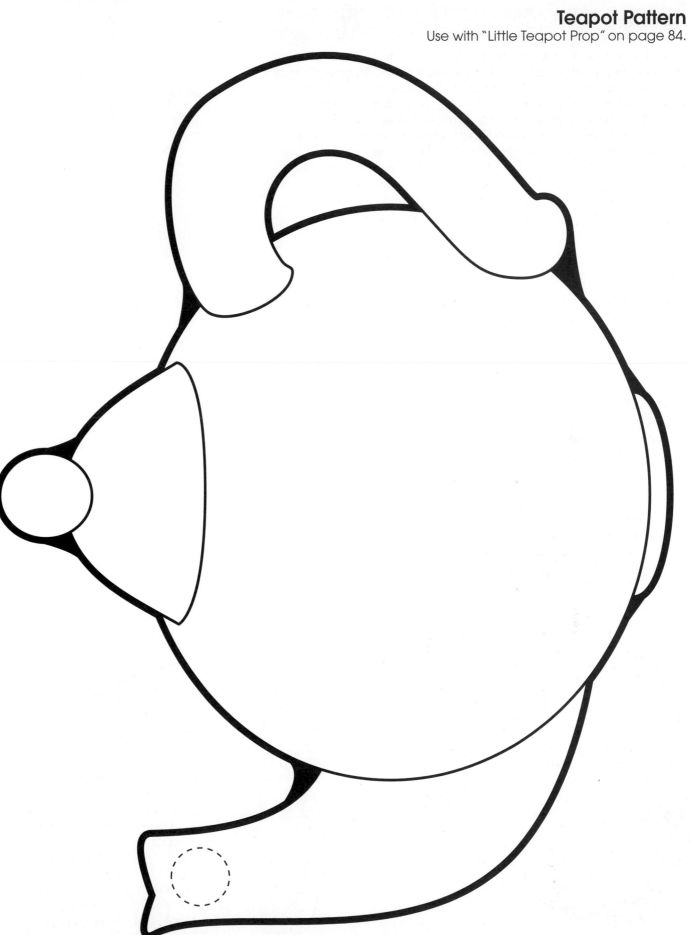

Under the Ground

Burrow into these curriculum-related activities to discover hidden wonders found under the ground.

ideas by Mackie Rhodes

Soil from:

Woods	Field	Planted Area
lots of crumbled leaves	sand	lots of roots
tiny sticks	tiny rocks	dark dirt
rocks	dead grass	bugs
bugs	pieces of plants	
roots	worms	
dried, broken pine needles		
pieces of pinecones		

Diggin' for Discoveries

Get the scoop on soil and introduce your youngsters to the world *under* the ground. To begin, gather hand shovels or sturdy spoons and several gallon-size zippered plastic bags. Take children outdoors and have them dig soil samples from each of several different areas around your school, such as an open field, a wooded area, and a landscaped area. Put each sample in a separate bag and label it. Back in the classroom, examine and discuss the contents of each bag, listing the comments on chart paper. Then compare the comments. What are the differences? The similarities?

Up Close and Magnified

Give youngsters a close-up, magnified view of soil; then have them create their own take-home magnifiers. To prepare, make ring tracers by following the steps in the illustration. Then cut out two 6½-inch circles of clear Con-Tact® covering for each child. Also, gather craft glue and a class supply of wide craft sticks and construction paper. To make a magnifier, have each child place the flat edge of a tracer on a construction paper fold, trace it, and then cut it out. Have him repeat the process to make another ring. Next, encourage each child to examine a soil sample (from "Diggin' for Discoveries") with a real magnifying glass. Afterward, instruct him to peel off the backing from his circles of clear covering. Have him sandwich a little bit of soil between the sticky sides of his circles. Finally, have him glue the lens between the two rings, inserting a craft stick between one ring and the lens. When the glue is dry, invite each child to take his magnifier home to share his soil discoveries with his family.

Ring Tracers

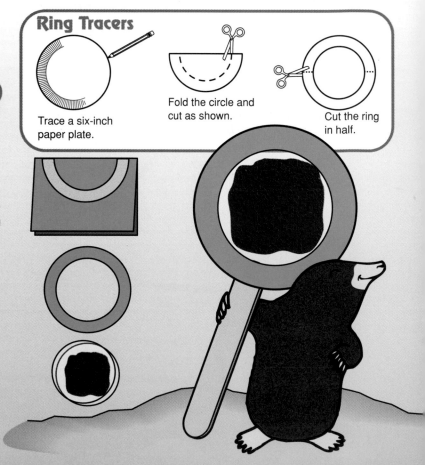

Trace a six-inch paper plate.

Fold the circle and cut as shown.

Cut the ring in half.

Underground Treasures

Colorful surprises are often found in rocks and stones under the ground. To reinforce the various colors of rocks—and lots of other skills—invite children to try their hands at this rockhounding activity. To prepare, mix a bag of colored aquarium gravel in your sand table and provide scoops and sieves. Then place a supply of clear plastic tumblers beside the table. To begin, students in a small group use the sieves to separate the gravel and sand. Then they sort the gravel into the tumblers by color. (For an added fine-motor twist, have children sort the gravel with tweezers.) If desired, add a kitchen scale to this center and encourage each child to guess which container of gravel weighs the most. Then have the students weigh each container to find out. Afterward, have the group mix the gravel back into the sand to prepare for the next group.

Veggies Down Under

Do your students know that there's a veritable vegetable feast growing under the ground? Bring in an assortment of fresh vegetables that grow underground, such as potatoes, carrots, turnips, beets, onions, and radishes. After the class examines the vegetables, cut several of them in half (but *not* the onions!). Then invite each child to make vegetable prints along the bottom of a large sheet of construction paper. When the paint is dry, have the artist smudge soil over the painting to resemble the ground. (Depending on the type of soil you have, you might need to rub a glue stick over the area before the soil is smudged on.) Invite each child to complete her picture by drawing an aboveground scene on her paper. Spray each child's completed picture with a light coat of hairspray to prevent it from smearing. Display the pictures with the title "Veggies Down Under."

Blooming Bulb Delight

This delectable underground snack contains an "edi-bulb" surprise! Before making it, show youngsters packaged bulbs, such as daffodils and tulips. Explain that each of these beautiful flowers grows from an underground bulb. Encourage students to examine the bulbs and the pictures of the flowers that grow from them. Then invite youngsters to wash up and dig into this fun snack activity.

Blooming Bulb Delight

(ingredients per child)

2 crushed chocolate sandwich cookies
1 serving instant chocolate pudding
1 candy spearmint leaf, cut in half lengthwise
1 candy fruit slice
1 unwrapped lollipop

Mix the cookies and pudding in a clear plastic tumbler. Then slide each green leaf onto the lollipop stick as shown. Top the stick with a fruit slice to resemble a flower blossom. Poke the lollipop into the pudding soil, leaving the leaves and flower above the soil. To eat, "pick" the flower. Nibble the bloom and leaves off the stem. Then use the bulb as a spoon. Finally, enjoy the lasting flavor of the tasty bulb.

Roly-Poly

The interesting little critter known as a *roly-poly* is one of many different kinds of animals that burrow underground. It also curls up into a small ball to protect itself. After sharing this information with youngsters, invite them to create their own curling roly-polies. To make one, cut a toilet paper tube in half lengthwise. Round the corners with scissors; then paint the half gray. When the paint is dry, cut five to seven wedges out of each side. Attach the hook side of a strip of self-adhesive Velcro® to the underside of one end, trapping the middle of a short length of black thread under it to make the antennae (as shown). Attach the corresponding strip of Velcro to the top of the other end of the body and lightly paint it gray. To curl the roly-poly, gently roll the ends toward each other, hooking the Velcro pieces together. Encourage youngsters to gently roll their curled up roly-polies across the floor. How about even measuring the distance traveled? Later, invite students to include their little critters in their dramatic-play activities in your block area. Roly-poly doodle all the day!

It's a Worm's World

Worms are another kind of animal that lives underground. To demonstrate how an underground worm burrow looks, have your class help set up this wormy experiment. To prepare, cut the top off of a two-liter soda bottle. For safety purposes, edge the rim of the bottle with masking tape. Then make a sleeve from a sheet of black construction paper (see diagram) to cover the bottle. To begin the experiment, fill the bottle three-quarters full with damp soil. Top the soil with moist, decaying leaves; then add a few worms. Cover the sleeved bottle with an inverted paper bag. Set the bottle aside in a dark, quiet place and leave it undisturbed for a day or two. Then remove the coverings to reveal the worm's world!

Dough Directions:

(enough for 3 to 4 children)

1 c. flour
1/2 c. salt
1/2 c. water
1/4 c. white glue

Mix together the flour, salt, water, and glue. Add more flour or water as needed until a soft dough is formed.

Underground "Con-doughs"

Ants, rabbits, moles, groundhogs, foxes, mice, and snakes—these are just a few of the many different animals that live in burrows. Some animals dig simple holes while others create extensive networks of tunnels and rooms. Invite each child to create a model of a burrow with this special recipe. To prepare the dough, follow the directions (left). To make a burrow, have each child roll out a 1/4-inch-xthick patty of dough on a sheet of tagboard. Then have her gently rub soil into her dough. Next, instruct her to use the side of a pencil and a soda bottle lid to create tunnels and rooms in the dough. When her model is dry (after several days), encourage the child to color the surrounding area of the tagboard. Spray each child's mat with hairspray to serve as a fixative. Then have youngsters use their mats for sorting and counting items that represent things related to burrowing animals, such as seeds (food), raisins (ants), or mini pom-poms (baby animals).

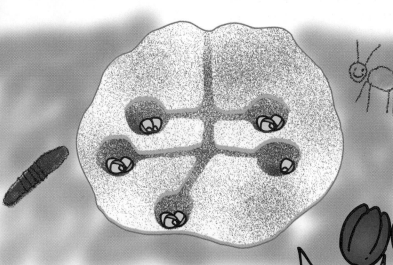

Take a Look Under the Ground

Teach youngsters this song to summarize your under-the-ground unit. Then encourage them to continue to explore the underground world in their daily outdoor activities.

(sung to the tune of "Twinkle, Twinkle, Little Star")

Take a look under the ground.
See what wonders can be found.
A roly-poly or a fox,
Sticks and roots, bulbs and rocks.
Rabbits, groundhogs, mice, and moles,
Earthworms, ants—all in their holes!

Veggies!

Beans, broccoli, corn, and carrots—feast on the thematic ideas in this unit that focus on the edible parts of plants.

ideas by Nancy M. Lotzer

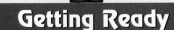

Veggie Sort

Sort out your class collection of vegetables with this small-group sorting idea. In advance, wash a vinyl tablecloth and lay it out on a flat surface. Then ask a small group of children to sort the vegetables on the tablecloth. Did they sort by color? Shape? Size? Can they think of another way to sort the vegetables?

? Did you know...
There are *purple* string beans!

Getting Ready

To prepare for your vegetable venture, make a class supply of the parent note on page 95. Send a copy home with each child. When the veggies have arrived, begin the activities. (If you are unable to get real vegetables, enlarge and photocopy the vegetable patterns on page 95. Color and laminate the patterns; then use them in the activities that follow.) There's no doubt that your students will grow and flower with vegetable knowledge!

Veggie Vocabulary

Teach your students the vegetable basics by introducing them to some veggie vocabulary. In advance, position a vinyl tablecloth in your read-aloud area. Gather your little ones together along with the class vegetable collection. Introduce vegetable vocabulary with a book such as *Oliver's Vegetables* by Vivian French (Orchard Books) and refer to "The Parts We Eat" (page 93). Afterward, use an index card to label a column on a vinyl tablecloth for each of the following: roots, tubers, stems, leaves, flowers, fruits, and seeds or pods. In turn, ask each child to choose a vegetable from the collection and put it in the appropriate section of the tablecloth (graph). When all the vegetables have been placed, read the labels together. Don't miss this opportunity to discuss what the graph reveals! (You also might like to have older students use copies of the patterns on page 95 to make individual pictorial representations of the real graph.)

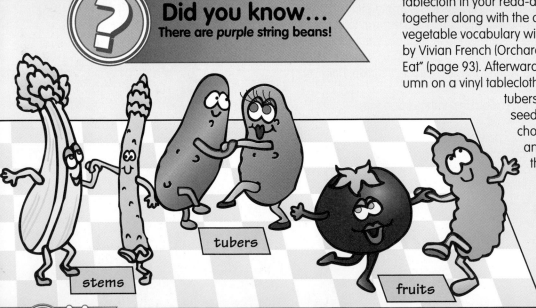

stems

tubers

fruits

The Parts We Eat

Roots—Some vegetables come from the roots of a plant. These are called *root vegetables*.
Examples: carrots, radishes

Tubers—Some vegetables form from special underground stems. These are called *tubers*.
Examples: potatoes, yams

Stems—Sometimes we eat the stems of a plant.
Examples: asparagus, celery

Leaves—Sometimes we eat the leaves of a plant.
Examples: lettuce, cabbage

Flowers—Sometimes we eat the flowering part of a plant.
Examples: broccoli, cauliflower

Fruits—Sometimes we eat the fruit of a plant.
Examples: tomatoes, cucumbers

Pods and seeds—Sometimes we eat the pods or seeds of a plant.
Examples: sweet corn, peas

Very Big Veggies

In your art area, provide cut raw vegetables (carrots, potatoes, etc.), newspaper or plastic grocery bags, bulletin board paper, scissors, a stapler, and paint. Then help each child follow the directions below to make her own pretend vegetable.

1. Cut out two identical vegetable shapes from bulletin board paper.
2. Use the art supplies to make prints and designs on them.
3. When the paint is dry, staple the vegetable halves together, leaving an opening for stuffing.
4. Gently stuff the vegetable with crumpled sheets of newspaper or plastic grocery bags. Finish stapling.
5. Add details for that particular vegetable, such as curling ribbon to the end of a green bean and narrow crepe paper strips to the top of a carrot.

Veggie Tune

(adapted to the tune of "Here We Go Looby Loo")

Some veggies are [red], it's true!
Some veggies are [brown], oh my!
Some veggies are [green], oh yes!
Did you ever give them a try?

Some veggies are [round], it's true!
Some veggies are [long], oh my!
Some veggies are [small], oh yes!
Did you ever give them a try?

Sing the song at left with your little ones to reinforce some simple veggie facts. Use student suggestions in place of the underlined words for a fun twist on the tune!

Vegetation Estimation

Enthuse your students with some math fun! In advance, purchase a bag of potatoes. Gather your youngsters in a circle and pass (or roll!) the bag of potatoes around for observation. Have each child guess how many potatoes are in the bag. Record the estimates on a sheet of chart paper. Then count the potatoes together and record the actual number on the chart. And then, of course, who could resist a round or two of Hot Potato? For added estimation practice, place various bagged vegetables at a center and invite students to estimate and then count the vegetables. Is anybody willing to tackle a bag of peas?

😊	❓	☹️
I like it!	Never tried it.	No, thank you.

Voting for Veggies!

Encourage your children to voice their opinions of vegetables…by voting! Beforehand, make a poster board chart as shown. Introduce the chart to your class, explaining each section. Then have each student cut out (or draw) different pictures of vegetables to glue to the chart, indicating her opinion. After each child has contributed to the chart, discuss the results. Hang the completed chart for all to see. Your little learners will be "rooting" for their favorite veggies!

Vegetable Tales

Delight your little ones with stories about oversized vegetables (see the list of suggestions below) and then watch your students' enthusiasm grow as they make their own giant veggies for your dramatic-play area (see "Very Big Veggies" on page 93).

Cucumber Soup
Written by Vickie Leigh Krudwig
Published by Fulcrum Publishing

The Giant Carrot
Written by Jan Peck
Published by Dial Books for Young Readers

The Enormous Potato
Retold by Aubrey Davis
Published by Kids Can Press

The Gigantic Turnip
Written by Aleksei Tolstoy
Published by Barefoot Books

Dear Parent,

We are learning about vegetables! To help us learn about these foods from plants, would you please send the checked vegetable (fresh, not canned) by _____?
(date)

___ asparagus   ___ broccoli   ___ green beans   ___ spinach
___ bag of carrots   ___ cauliflower   ___ lettuce   ___ tomatoes
___ bag of potatoes   ___ celery   ___ onions   ___ turnips
___ bell peppers   ___ corn on the cob   ___ radishes   ___ your choice

Thanks for your support in education!

©2000 The Education Center, Inc. • *Themes From A to Z* • TEC373

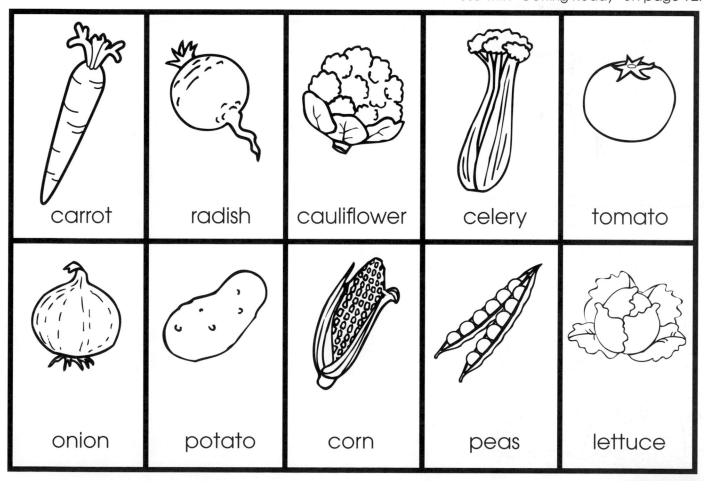

| carrot | radish | cauliflower | celery | tomato |
| onion | potato | corn | peas | lettuce |

Wonderful Wheels

Around and around and around they go! Students will roll right along as they learn all about wheels.

ideas by Theresa Knapp

Why Wheels?

Get your little ones in gear with this critical-thinking group activity. Begin by asking students to brainstorm a list of things that have wheels. Then ask them to imagine what it would be like (on a farm, in a city, at a park, etc.) without wheels. Guide children to state how important wheels are in our lives. As a follow-up, have students look through magazines and cut out pictures of wheels. Then provide a sheet of poster board and some glue. Invite each child to glue his pictures onto the poster to make one big class collage of wheels.

The Wheels on the...

Sure, the wheels on the *bus* go round and round. But what do other types of wheels do? In advance, enlarge and copy the vehicle patterns on page 99. Color the pictures, cut them apart, and back them with tagboard or construction paper. Laminate each picture if desired. After a rousing reading of *The Wheels on the Bus* by Paul Zelinsky, get your students moving with a related song. Place each vehicle card facedown. Have one child pick up a card and then tell the class which vehicle is on the card. Then ask the class to describe what those particular wheels might do. (Would they go fast? Would you find them on a track? Are they big?) Next, sing and act out the song below, replacing the underlined words with the children's responses. (See the list for suggestions.) Repeat the song until every card has been selected.

(adapted to the tune of "The Wheels on the Bus")

The wheels on the [fire truck] [go fast, fast, fast],
   [fast, fast, fast], [fast, fast, fast].
The wheels on the [fire truck] [go fast, fast, fast],
All through the town!

train—go on the track
truck—are big and fat
tractor—are oh so big
plane—go screech, screech, screech
wagon—go wobble, wobble, wobble

Wearable Wheels

Those little *thinking* wheels will be turning with this pattern necklace activity! In advance, dye a large supply of wheel-shaped pasta (use at least three different colors). Then cut a necklace length of yarn for each student. Knot one end of each yarn length around a pasta wheel. Arrange the colored pasta and yarn in a center. Invite each child to string the wheels onto her piece of yarn, creating a pattern. Then tie the yarn to make a necklace. Whee! Wearable wheels!

Make Way for Wheels!

Welcome wheeled vehicles into your classroom with these creative works of art! To make one, cut a cube tissue box in half; then trim it as desired. Securely tape two nonbendable straws to the bottom of the box for axles. Then insert a long pipe cleaner into each straw. Slip an empty spool onto the end of each pipe cleaner; then bend each pipe cleaner to secure the spools in place. Decorate the vehicle by gluing on craft gems or sequins to resemble lights and other details. To make seats, glue one-third of an egg carton bottom into the box. To make a family, use permanent markers to draw faces on plastic eggs. Then give each family member a seat! If desired, have your students create ramps, bridges, and tunnels for the vehicles. Your little ones will delight in driving, bumping, and racing around your dramatic-play area!

Creative Cracker Creations

Your students will be bumper to bumper waiting in line to make these creative cracker snacks. To prepare, you'll need paper plates and an assortment of cracker types and shapes, such as whole graham crackers; small, square cheese crackers; round crackers; and oyster crackers. Have each child write her name on a paper plate; then encourage her to use the crackers to create her own wheeled vehicle on the plate. Once each child has made a vehicle, arrange the vehicles in a display and invite students to look at one another's creative cracker creations. There will be lots of oohs and aahs before the typical crunching and munching of snacktime!

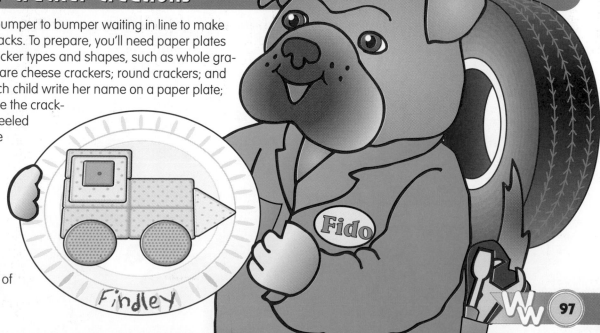

Findley

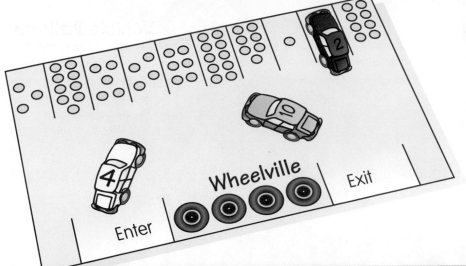

Welcome to Wheelville!

Wheelville needs some help! The towns-people have forgotten where to park! Your little ones can come to their rescue with a game that reinforces math skills in a "wheely" fun way! On a large sheet of poster board, create and label a parking lot with dots as shown. Use toy cars labeled with numbers that correspond to the dots in the parking spaces. Then have each student park the vehicles in their proper parking spaces. Wheels are so much fun!

Wheels of Art

Little mechanics will love making these wheelable art projects! To prepare the cars, punch holes where indicated (with a dot) on the cars and the wheels. Use a craft knife to cut a $3/4$-inch slit at the bottom of the front window on each car. To start the project, have each student color and cut out a car and two wheels. Help each child insert each length of pipe cleaner through a different hole in the car, bending the ends to secure them to the back of the car. Next, instruct each child to slide the wheels onto the pipe cleaners and bend the pipe cleaners to keep the wheels in place. Invite each child to decorate her craft spoon and then slide it into the window slit. If desired, have students make another set of colored wheels so that the tires can be changed. Beep, beep! Little mechanics on the go!

For each child:
1 tagboard copy of the car pattern
    and 2 wheel patterns (page 99)
two 3" lengths of pipe cleaner
crayons
scissors
wooden craft spoon

For teacher preparation:
hole puncher
craft knife

Bears on Wheels

By Stan and Jan Berenstain
Published by Random House, Inc.

Wheel on into counting skills with this literature-based activity. To prepare, label seven paper plates with the following numerals: 0, 1, 2, 3, 4, 5, and 10. Next, draw wheels on each plate to correspond with the numerals. Gather bear counters and then invite students to sit in a circle around the plates. Read the story, stopping after each page so that a student can use the bears to demonstrate what the page has related. Finally, place the book, bears, and plates at a center so that your little ones can act out the story on their own.

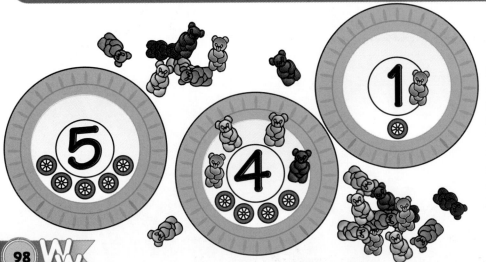

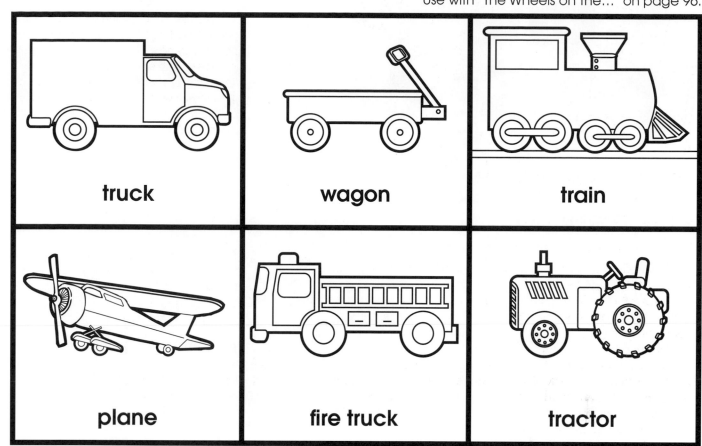

truck

wagon

train

plane

fire truck

tractor

Use with "Wheels of Art" on page 98.

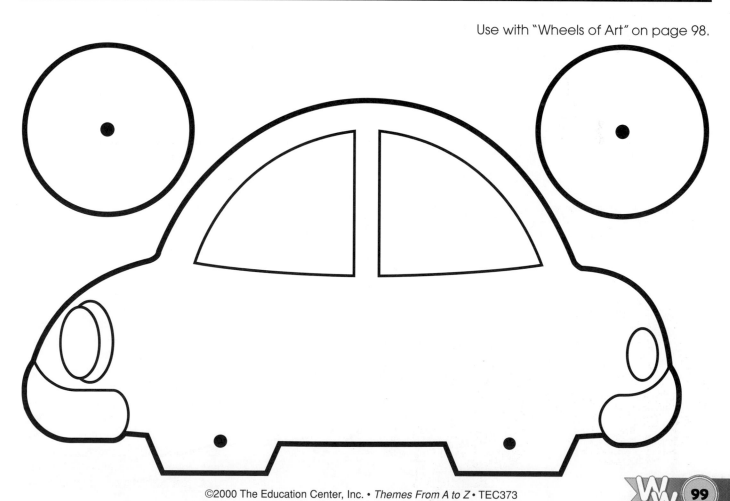

X Marks the Spot

Use these cross-curricular X activities to explore beginning map skills and all kinds of excellent learning activities.

ideas by Anita Ortiz

X Marks the Spot on Me!

This X marks the spot for art and exercise! To prepare, cut out a class supply of tagboard Xs. Have each child color his X and use art supplies to decorate it as desired. Then have him make a handle by gluing a wide craft stick to the back of the X. When the glue is dry, begin your exercise extravaganza! Instruct children to stand in a circle. Call out a variety of patterned directions such as those listed below. Invite students to use their Xs to mark the spots you name. To extend this activity, ask child volunteers to make up patterned directions and call them out. Then have the whole class join in on the pattern.

Direction suggestions:
"X marks the spot—head, shoulders, toes, head, shoulders, toes…"
"X marks the spot—tummy, nose, nose, tummy, nose, nose…"
"X marks the spot—toe, heel, heel, elbow, toe, heel, heel, elbow…"

School Excursions

Develop map and thinking skills with this X-marks-the-spot activity! Beforehand, enlarge a simple map of your school. Then trace the basics onto a sheet of bulletin board paper and label it as desired. For added visual cues, glue photos to corresponding places on the map; then laminate it. Post the map near your classroom door where students can easily reach it. Before leaving on an excursion (lunch, the gym, etc.), have a child use a wipe-off marker to draw a line on the map starting from your classroom and ending with an X at your intended destination. Not only will your class know where they are going, but others will know where you are when you're away! X does mark the spot!

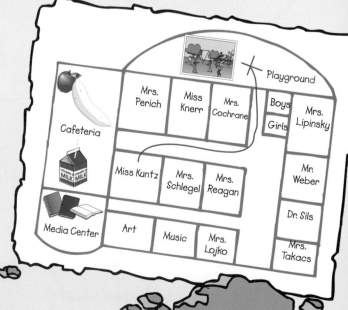

Where's the Spot?

Reinforce listening skills with this simple and fun activity. Beforehand, make a poster board spot. Then cut out two identical felt *X*s, stapling them together as shown. Insert a small dowel between the two *X*s to make a wand (gluing it in place if desired). To do this activity, have one child close her eyes. Then hide the spot. Have the child open her eyes, and give her the *X* wand. Ask her to find the hidden spot. As she moves about the classroom, invite the rest of the class to call out directions (according to students' abilities, you might use *hot* and *cold*, *left* and *right*, prepositional phrases, or even cardinal directions as clues). When the spot is found, have the child tap it with the *X* wand. Extend this activity by encouraging children to do it in small groups during center time. Where *is* that spot?

North

Here I am!

Where is North?

Where Is North?

Reinforce cardinal directions with this melodic little activity. In advance, post a sign for each cardinal direction on the corresponding wall of your classroom. Also tape a laminated *X* in the center of your room. Familiarize students with the signs; then choose one or more children to stand on (or near) the *X*. Ask the remaining children to stand under one of the four directional signs. Teach the song below, encouraging children to sing their corresponding parts. After singing the song four times, have children switch places and begin again.

(sung to the tune of "Where Is Thumbkin?")

Child(ren) on *X*:	Where is [North]? Where is [North]?
[North] students:	Here I am! Here I am!
Child(ren) on *X*:	How are you today, [North]?
[North] students:	Very well, I thank you.
Child(ren) on *X*:	So long [North]! So long [North]!
	(Children wave.)

South

Books About Beginning Map Skills

As the Crow Flies: A First Book of Maps
By Gail Hartman
Published by Aladdin Books

My Map Book
By Sara Fanelli
(Check your school or local libary.)

May I Have Directions, Please?

Here's a fun game that keeps everyone thinking! To begin, put a laminated construction paper X somewhere in your classroom. Stand a good distance away from the X and say to your class, "May I have directions, please?" In turn, have each child give you a verbal direction leading you to the X. Once you reach the X (and have modeled the activity sufficiently), put the X in a new location and choose a child to stand away from it. Then start round two! May I have directions, please?

Take two steps up!

X Marks Spot

In this activity, X marks Spot—the dog! Enlarge the pattern on page 103 and photocopy it several times. According to your children's abilities, write a different letter or word on each of Spot's spots. Make a master list of each letter or word used. Use the same letters or words to program the remaining Spot patterns, but write them in a different order. Then make a class supply of the patterns. To play, give each child in a small group a copy of Spot. Call out a letter or word. Have each student write an X on the corresponding spot. When students have Xs on all the spots, they call out together "X marks my Spot!"

Treasure Map

Culminate your "X Marks the Spot" unit with a treasure map that leads to real treasure! On a paper grocery bag, draw a map of your playground with a dotted path leading to a large X. Wrap gold candy coins (or other small items) for each student and place them in the chosen area on the playground. Crumple the map slightly to look worn, roll it up, and then tie it to a tree or outside bench for easy discovery. When your little ones go out to play and find the map, watch their excitement grow as you all follow the map to find the treasure. What a perfect ending to an "X-traordinary" unit!

Spot Pattern

Use with "*X* Marks Spot" on page 102.

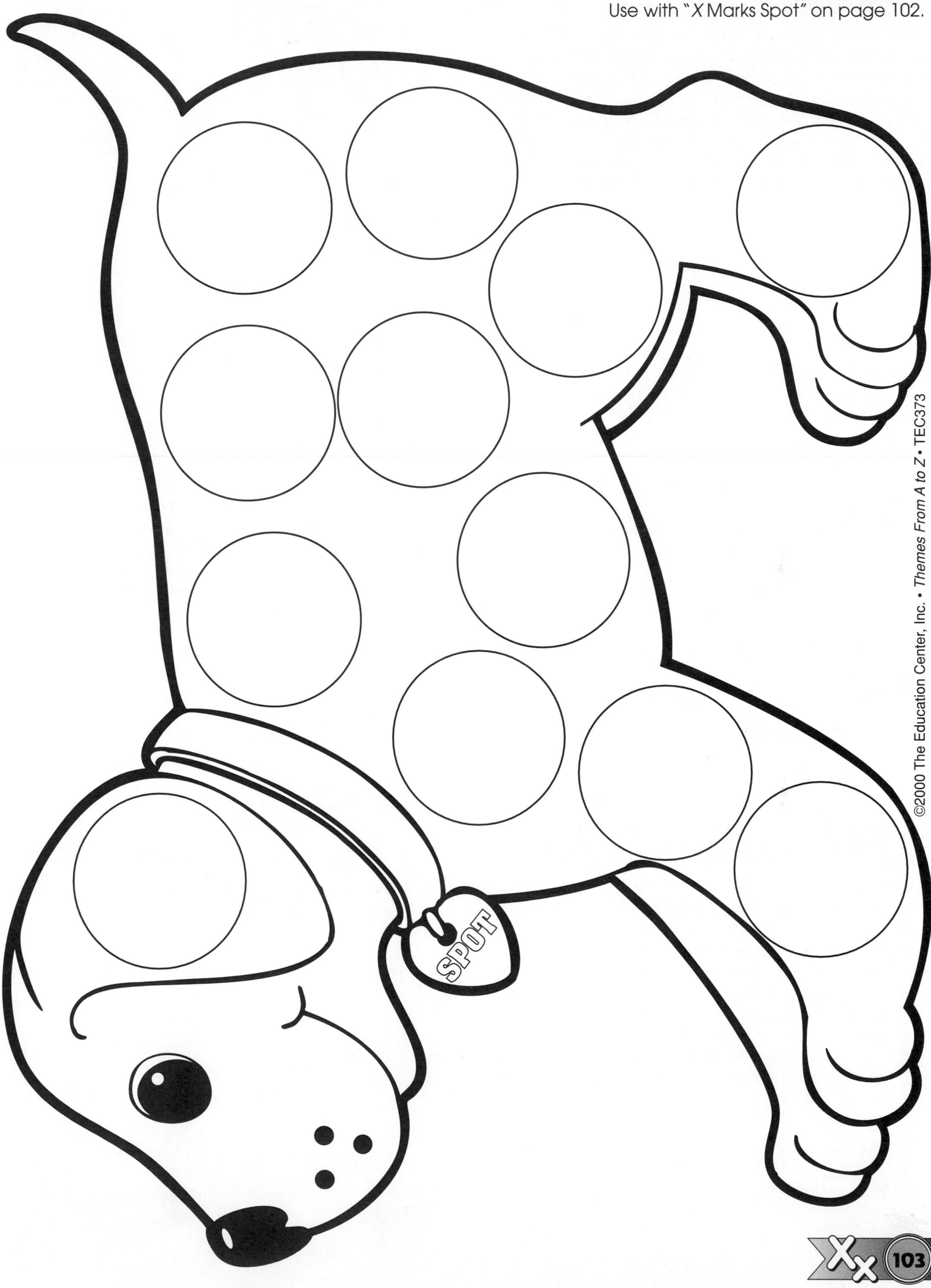

Hello, Yellow!

Brighten your youngsters' learning fun with these cross-curricular activities related to the color yellow.

ideas contributed by Suzanne Moore

Yellow Song

Sing a song of yellow! Teach the song below to your children. At the end of the song, point to two children who have their hands raised. Ask both of them to stand and name something yellow. Have those two children sit down; then invite the whole class to sing the song again with the new child-suggested ideas. Keep going until you run out of yellow!

(adapted to the tune of "This Old Man")

[Lemons] [is/are] yellow.
[Apples] can be too.
I like yellow
And I like you!
If you think of something yellow,
Please raise your hand.
When I point to you,
Would you please stand?

Yellow Twins

Highlight the color yellow all around your classroom with this visual-discrimination game. To prepare, collect a supply of identical pairs of yellow objects, such as crayons, blocks, pencils, counters, construction paper, silk flowers, and toy dishes. Put one item from each pair in a bag. Then hide the remaining items around your room. To play, chant the rhyme below. When you say the last line, remove an item from the bag and give it to a child. Ask that child to search the room to find the matching item. Repeat the activity until all of the yellow pairs are matched; then arrange the matched pairs in a yellow display. Later, put the bag and yellow pairs in a center for youngsters to use in their own versions of this game.

Look around the classroom
To see what you can see.
Can you find my yellow twin?
It looks just like me!

Substitutions for "Yellow Song":
The sun, canaries; Our blocks, Jell-O®;
Sunflowers, crayons; Bananas, dogs;
My raincoat, baby chicks; Cornbread,
mustard; Scrambled eggs, pudding

I can be a beach ball.

I can be a monster with a big yellow head!

Yellow Circle, Yellow Circle

Creativity is the name of the game when youngsters write and illustrate this fascinating class book. To prepare, cut out a large supply of various sizes of yellow circles. Glue one or more of the circles to a construction paper cover and title it "Yellow Circle, Yellow Circle, What Can You Be?" Show youngsters a yellow circle and ask them to brainstorm some things that might be created from that circle, such as a sunny-day scene, a bicycle, or a monster! Afterward, provide crayons, markers, and a sheet of construction paper for each child. Instruct each child to choose a yellow circle and create a picture that incorporates the circle. When he finishes, write his dictation on the page. Then stack all the pages and staple them behind the construction paper cover. During group time, read the title of the book together; then have the author of the first page share his creation with the class. Continue in this manner, reciting the title of the book before each person shares his page. Later, store the book in your class library for free-time reading.

From Bright to Light

Enlighten your students with this small-group color study about yellow. To prepare, make a class supply of the recording form on page 107. For each small group of students, label each of six clear plastic cups with a numeral from 1 to 6. Pour a one-fourth cup of yellow paint into each cup. To begin your study, point out the bright color of the yellow paint in each cup. Set cup 1 aside; then have a child stir one tablespoon of white paint into cup 2. Ask another child to stir two tablespoons of white paint into cup 3. Continue in this manner, adding an additional spoonful of white paint to each consecutive cup. Then ask youngsters to paint the cups on their recording forms with each corresponding color. Have them compare the different *tints* of yellow on their papers; then explain that these are called tints because white paint was added to the yellow. Afterward, invite each child to paint pictures or designs with the different tints created by her group.

Name Charlie

Paint Recording Form

Color study

1   2   3

4   5   6

Yellow Hideaway

Bring the beautiful yellow blooms of the sunflower right into your classroom to create this inviting hideaway. First, share *Sunflower House* by Eve Bunting (Harcourt Brace & Company). Then invite each child to make a sunflower for a class sunflower house. To make a flower, have a child glue 2½" lengths of yellow crepe paper around the edge of a plate. Then have him glue unshelled sunflower seeds onto the center of his plate. When the glue is dry, instruct him to turn the plate over and glue 3" lengths of green crepe paper around the back edge of the plate. To create the house, drape and tape white bulletin board paper over the top and three sides of a large table. Then use rolled masking tape to attach the flowers to the walls and roof of the house. Invite children to visit the floral retreat for some quiet reading or napping.

Yellow Yummies

Delight youngsters with an array of yellow taste treats. Simply prepare an assortment of yellow foods, such as the ones listed below. Then put each one in a separate dish along with a serving utensil. Provide plastic plates, forks, and spoons; then invite each child to select and sample the yellow yummies of his choice.

- pineapple slices (or chunks)
- lemon yogurt
- cornbread mini muffins
- cubed yellow apples
- banana slices (served with the skin on)
- yellow popcorn

Luscious Lemon Punch

Little fingers will get a fine-motor workout when youngsters mix up this fizzy yellow concoction. You will need a lemon juicer, a bowl, a measuring cup, lemon-lime soda, and lemon sherbet. For each child, you will also need a lemon half, a clear plastic cup, a straw, and a spoon. To make the punch, each child juices her lemon on the juicer, discards the seeds, and pours the juice into her cup. Then she adds a half cup of lemon-lime soda to her lemon juice. Finally, she tops off her drink with a heaping table-spoon of lemon sherbet—watch out for the foam!

Books About Yellow

The Emperor Who Hated Yellow
By Jim Edmiston
Published by Barefoot Books, Inc.

Little Blue and Little Yellow
By Leo Lionni
Published by Scholastic Inc.

Yolanda's Yellow School
By Kelly Asbury
Published by Henry Holt and Company

Paint Recording Form

Black-and-White and "Outta" Sight

Tell your students to put on their pith helmets and hiking boots because they are going to the African savanna to catch a glimpse of some wild striped zebras!

ideas by Ellen Van De Walle

Zebras
are black and white
are animals
are furry
have four legs
look like horses
are wild
are sometimes at zoos
are striped

Becoming Zebra Experts

Zip right into your zebra theme by having your youngsters create an information chart. Display a picture of a zebra near your circle-time area and then gather your students. Encourage each child to hold up a pair of imaginary binoculars and closely examine the zebra picture. Have each student tell you about what he observes. Record each response on a piece of chart paper as shown. When everyone has had a turn to share his thoughts, read or paraphrase *The Zebra: Striped Horse* by Christine Denis-Huot (Charlesbridge Publishing, Inc.). Then encourage your students to add more information to their chart. Finally, reread the chart to review what your students now know about these unique striped animals!

Zany Zebras

Your little learners will be full of zeal as they create an African savanna mural complete with zebras! In advance, enlarge the zebra pattern on page 111 to make several tagboard templates. On a large sheet of bulletin board paper, have each student take a turn painting something found on a savanna, such as a tree, a shrub, a water hole, tall grass, clouds, or the sun. While the paintings dry, give each student a newspaper page (place it in front of her with the text in a vertical position) and have her use a black crayon to trace or color around a zebra template. Help each child cut out her zebra shape before adding lengths of black yarn or ribbon for a mane and a tail. Then have your little ones glue their zebras onto the mural. There you have it—a zany zebra display!

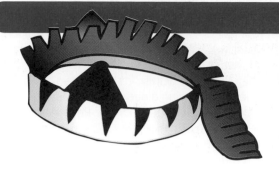

Zebra Wear

Invite youngsters to transform themselves into zebras when they don these fun black-and-white headbands. To make a headband, use a black crayon to make stripes on a 2" x 20" strip of white poster board. Glue two black construction paper triangles to the headband to resemble a zebra's ears. Staple the ends of the strip together to fit the child's head. Next, tape a fringed 3" x 20" strip of black construction paper to the center front and center back of the headband as shown. Encourage little ones to put on their headbands for the following activity. Ready, zebras? Let's go!

A Herd of Playful Zebras

Who's that zigzagging about your room? It's your students, pretending to be a herd of zebras! Arrange your youngsters (wearing the headbands described in "Zebra Wear") in a circle and then select one child to be the zebra. Have the group chant the first verse of the rhyme below as the selected zebra gallops around the outside of the circle. When the verse has ended, have the zebra choose another child from the herd to join him. Chant the verse again, this time saying *two, zebras,* and *they* in place of the underlined words. Continue in this manner until your whole herd is galloping about! Then chant the final verse and have your children act out the movements. What fun!

Zebra Rhyme
(chanted to the rhythm of "One Elephant Went Out to Play")

[One] little [zebra] went out to play
On the savanna one fine day.
[He] had such enormous fun
[He] asked another zebra to come!

The zebra herd went out to play
On the savanna one fine day.
They grew tired as they ran around
So they all lay down!

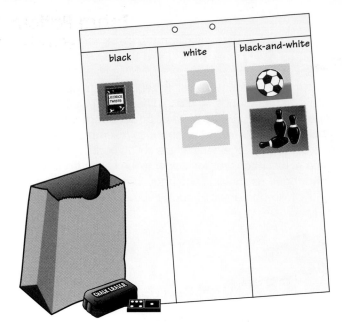

What Am I?

Prompt youngsters' critical-thinking skills with this black-and-white guessing game! Select a variety of black, white, and black-and-white items; then put them in a paper grocery bag. Before beginning the activity, introduce a variety of black-and-white objects by reading aloud *Animals: Black and White* by Phyllis Limbacher Tildes (Charlesbridge Publishing, Inc.) or *Dylan's Day Out* by Peter Catalanotto (Orchard Books). Then give your students clues about each item in your bag. For example, for a marshmallow you might say, "This item is white and soft and sweet to eat." Allow students to guess each item's identity. When all of the items are revealed, label three vertical columns on a sheet of chart paper as shown. Then have your students look through magazines and catalogs searching for pictures that belong in the three categories. Have a child use a glue stick to glue each picture in the correct column on the chart.

Striped Sandwiches

Zoom in on zebras during snacktime with these tasty treats! Use a horse cookie cutter to cut zebra shapes from slices of bread. Have each student spread softened cream cheese onto his zebra. Then have him use raisins, brown M&M's Minis®, or mini chocolate chips to add stripes. These striped sandwiches are sure to satisfy!

My Own Zebra Book

Your little ones can show off their knowledge of zebras when they make these informative booklets. In advance, duplicate the cover on page 111 for each child. Then program a half sheet of white copy paper for each booklet page, using the boldfaced text below. Duplicate each programmed sheet to make a class supply. Following a review of students' zebra knowledge, guide each student in illustrating her zebra booklet pages and cover as suggested. Have her glue her cover to a half-sheet of construction paper. Stack each child's finished pages beneath her cover and staple along the left side. Your youngsters will be delighted to take these books home and share zebra facts with their family members!

Cover: Write your name on the line. Color scenery.
Page 1: **Zebras are _____.** Draw a zebra. Use short pieces of black and white pipe cleaner pieces to make stripes on the zebra's body. Then dictate a word or phrase to fill in the blank.
Page 2: **Here is where they live.** Draw a zebra's natural habitat. *(trees, grass, water hole, sun)*
Page 3: **This is what zebras like to eat.** Glue on strips of yellow and green tissue paper to resemble long grass.
Page 4: **Some zebras have brown stripes!** Draw a zebra with brown stripes.
Page 5: **I like zebras because _____.** Draw a black-and-white zebra. Dictate a phrase to fill in the blank.

Zebra Pattern
Use with "Zany Zebras" on page 108.

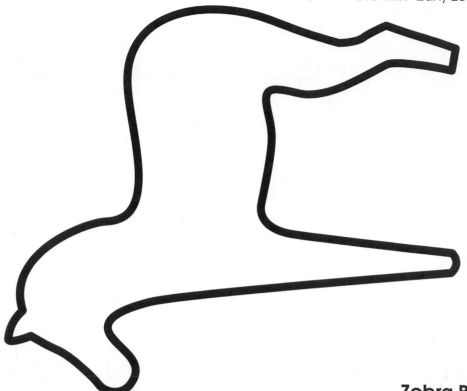

Zebra Booklet Cover
Use with "My Own Zebra Book" on page 110.

by _____

©2000 The Education Center, Inc. • *Themes From A to Z* • TEC373

Planning Form

Theme: _____   Date: _____

Circle Time

Movement Time

Center Time

Snacktime

Rhythm-and-Rhyme Time

Outdoor Time

Project Time

Small-Group Time

Storytime